LIBERATING JESUS

LIBERATING JESUS

BY
ROBERTA GRIMES

Liberating Jesus
by: Roberta Grimes

Publisher's Cataloging-In-Publication Data
(Prepared by The Donohue Group, Inc.)
Names: Grimes, Roberta.
Title: Liberating Jesus / by Roberta Grimes.
Description: Madison, VA : Christine F. Anderson Publishing & Media, [2015]
Identifiers: ISBN 978-0-692-54281-1 (paperback) | ISBN 978-0-692-26423-2 (ebook)
Subjects: LCSH: Revelation. | Jesus Christ. | Spiritualism. | Christianity. | Spiritual life. | Bible--Criticism, interpretation, etc.
Classification: LCC BT127.3 .G75 2015 (print) | LCC BT127.3 (ebook) | DDC 231.7/4--dc23

Published by
Christine F. Anderson Publishing & Media, Madison VA, 22727
www.cfapublishing.com

CHRISTINE F. ANDERSON

ISBN: 978-0692542811

Printed in the United States of America

Cover Photo credit: anastasia island sunrise, 16 december 2013
(http://www.flickr.com/photos/96518004@N02/11401823823) via http://photopin.com

This book is lovingly dedicated
to humanity's greatest Teacher

TABLE OF CONTENTS

"If you hold to my teaching, you are really my disciples. Then you will know the truth, and the truth will set you free."

(JN 8:31–32)

Writing this book was not my idea. Telling you how it came to be written was the farthest thing from what I wanted to do, so the fact that I am sharing it with you and also telling you where it came from is testimony to the fact that I am convinced it was written at the Lord's direction. I am told that Jesus has chosen this moment, two thousand years after He last walked the earth, to shed what He calls a corrupted Christian wrapper and again reveal His teachings to the world.

If this isn't the Second Coming you were looking for, please understand that I share your confusion. Over decades, I have been dragged away from the Christianity that I loved and made to understand that my religion is so different from what the Lord intended that I would have to make a choice. I could be a Christian or I could follow Jesus. I chose Jesus. That was when things began to get interesting.

To answer what was my biggest question, so you might be wondering about it as well: yes. I have it on good authority that Jesus is related to God in a way that you and

I are not, which is why in this book I have capitalized His pronouns. I am told that God chose to incarnate as the physical Jesus in an effort to understand how allowing humankind to have free will could possibly have gone so wrong. God as Jesus told us how to put human life on a better track, and He gave us that wisdom in concepts so simple that even first-century people could understand them. Now Jesus is reiterating His Gospel teachings two thousand years later because the custodians of those teachings have encased them in an easy, but meaningless, shortcut.

The answer to what may be your second biggest question if you are a Christian is: no. This book about freeing the teachings of Jesus from their religious wrapper is not the work of Satan. I am confident of this fact because:

1. In more than a century of looking for it, no afterlife researcher of whom I am aware has found evidence for an actual Satan. Indeed, the consciousness-based physics that governs all of reality and will dominate the second half of this century seems to make it impossible for a powerful evil entity to exist.

2. In April of 2009, I gave my life to God. This is an exercise that I recommend, but I have found

that very few will do it for fear that God might want them to do something unpleasant. Happily, that has not been my experience. Earnestly seeking and following God's guidance is the most fun I have had in my life.

3. If it actually is Satan's will that we free Jesus from the Christian wrapper and begin to follow His teachings perfectly, then you've got to think that maybe Satan isn't so awful after all. (I'm kidding! There is no Satan.)

Appendix V is the story of how this book came to be written. Here I will just say that apparently the civilization we are watching decline is on a course to disaster. Two hundred years from now, a climactic religious war is slated to be started by people who call themselves Christians (believe it or not). Some of those who believe that the entire Christian Bible is the Inspired Word of God are looking even now for the unblemished red heifer, the Rapture, and the gathering of the End Times armies. Eventually, they will run out of patience and start Armageddon on their own.

I find this prediction unbelievable! For anyone who has read the Gospel words of Jesus to believe that the Biblical Book of Revelation is anything more than the ravings of a man driven insane by persecution defies common sense. The End Times, Armageddon, and the Final Judgment? All of that is anathema to Jesus. Read your Gospels! Jesus is the Prince of Peace. But unless we can move quickly to assist Him in spreading His Gospel teachings to the world, apparently there still will be people two hundred years from now who will think that in destroying God's creation, they will be fulfilling God's plan.

I am told that the Lord's twenty-first-century project of bringing His teachings to all of humankind is going to be the work of many willing people. He calls His teachings a philosophy. It is His intention to free us from religious superstitions and teach us to relate to God on our own. And His teachings are meant to be followed by every person on the face of the earth. If we can help everyone of every religion to understand that Jesus is not a religious figure, but rather He is our universal Teacher, then I have it on good authority that the predicted end-times war can be averted. Civilization can restore and perfect itself, and our grandchildren's great-great-great-grandchildren will be born into what we are promised will be a heaven on earth. It is those who are born in this century who will determine whether human life will be worth living in the twenty-third century. And even whether there will be a twenty-third century.

If you are not a Christian, you can skip the first four chapters. Simply read the rest of this book as the beautiful teachings of a Prophet who is augmenting whatever you already believe with a philosophy that can help you live your own best life both now and forevermore. And, not incidentally, if sufficient people will follow this philosophy, then your descendants can have descendants of their own.

If you are a Christian, I understand that I am giving you a lot to process. I urge you to do what I have done, and read the Gospel red letters repeatedly. Spend time on your knees with an open heart. The only thing that ever could have induced me to leave the religion I loved was the persistent call of the Lord Himself. If it is His will that you now join Him in His effort to enlighten the world, then I expect that He will call you, too.

I used to say that my boss was a Jewish carpenter. But now I realize that my Boss is considerably more important: He is the Son of Man, God's presence on earth in human form. Whether my Boss is going to be your Boss, or whether you will continue to believe that being religious works best for you, is a decision that only God can help you make.

INTRODUCTION

When I was eight years old, I had a spiritual experience that led me to spend a half-century studying nearly two hundred years of afterlife evidence. There is so much of this evidence of so many kinds, and it is so entirely consistent, that eventually I was able to make sense of what is a gigantic picture! In 2010, I published *The Fun of Dying – Find Out What Really Happens Next*. Soon I was meeting others who also had undertaken this research, and I found to my wonderment that all of us had arrived at the same complex and beautiful conclusions. The study of death and the afterlife is a robust nascent science as real and objective as any other science. This is the century in which it is going to enrich every beautiful human life.

For ardent followers of Jesus, what we continue to learn about the afterlife is great validation. As you will see, what Jesus says in the Gospels is amazingly consistent with what we are learning from those more recently dead. Such extensive correspondence would be impossible if Jesus had not actually lived and been who He claims to be, so—praise God!—now we have both corroboration of the afterlife evidence and solid confirmation of the historical Jesus.

But as practicing Christians, we have a problem. While Jesus is right, it turns out that the core tenets of Christianity are wrong. In decades of seeking confirmation of specific Christian traditions, neither I nor any other researcher of whom I am aware has found evidence of any of the following:

1. That a human-like God exists.

2. That a powerful evil figure opposing God exists, or is possible.

3. That eternal damnation to a fiery hell ever has happened to anyone.

4. That the death of Jesus on the cross ever has saved anyone from anything.

5. That being a Christian matters when it comes to getting into heaven.

Basically, we can demonstrate now that Christianity is altogether wrong.

What I am telling you is true. Some who love Christianity might say we would have been better off without these discoveries, but the truth cannot be unlearned now. And, as you will see, there is evidence that in learning what is true we are following the calling of the

Lord and making possible the advent of God's Kingdom on earth.

The fact that Jesus is genuine while Christianity is man-made makes getting the truth out a matter of some urgency. Within the next few decades, communication between this level of reality and the areas where the dead reside will become so easy that what the dead know will become readily available to us. And it is going to be impossible for a Christianity that preaches sacrificial redemption and hellfire and the literal truth of the Christian Bible to survive the post-death testimony of those who know better. My fear is that by the end of this century, traditional Christianity will be in sharp decline, and we must make sure that people won't throw away our precious Baby with what is apparently bathwater.

I still love the Christianity I used to practice. I can sing so many hymns by heart! And the comfort of knowing that just by being the right kind of Christian I was on God's A-list is something I so fondly remember. But in compensation for my lost faith, I have found a glorious certainty. I have learned that Jesus is more important than I ever in my wildest dreams imagined, and God's plan for what is possible on earth is more wonderful than the human mind can dream.

My purpose here is not to convince you of anything. My purpose is simply to share with you what Jesus is asking that I share with you. For most of my life I was an earnest Christian, so when I began to discover the things that I discuss in this book, I was horrified. When I felt compelled to write *The Fun of Dying*, which includes some of this information, I prayed that God would please take me now if that book should not be published. All I want is that God's will be done! And God in the person of Jesus has had to speak to me quite specifically in order to convince me to write this book. I do it in service. Whether it upsets you or delights you, I ask that you accept it as the work of someone who gave her life to God in 2009 and has found to her ongoing wonderment that when you do that, God takes you at your word.

Understanding Our Dilemma

CHAPTER ONE
THE AFTERLIFE EVIDENCE IS IRREFUTABLE

I am astonished to realize how ignorant most people still are of what happens at and after death. The afterlife is too often considered to be a matter of belief, but it is not a matter of belief any more than your chair is a matter of belief. Your chair exists, and you can prove its existence by sitting down and not landing on the floor. That same sort of certainty pertains to life after death. Believing or not believing in this or that detail of it does not change what is objective reality.

My childhood experiences of light (see Appendix IV) made me know that more exists than what we see. They kindled in me a need to understand what those experiences had been, and the only way I could think to research events that remain vivid in my mind even a half-century later was to investigate the afterlife. Patiently, and over decades, that has been my engrossing hobby. What happened to me was real. I wanted a real explanation for it, so I have approached my attempt to understand what actually is going on with a pronounced degree of skepticism. Most afterlife researchers are skeptics, actually. We are assembling what we can see are bits of an enormous picture, and we won't accept anything as evidence unless it can be demonstrated to be objectively genuine.

THE EVIDENCE

Much of the evidence of what happens at and after death is personal to one or to just a few people, so it goes without saying that no single story, and no group of stories, can be considered trustworthy. But when hundreds of such stories are studied as a whole and are combined with other kinds of evidence, an enormous and stunningly consistent picture begins to form before our eyes. The fact that all the evidence can be made to fit together so perfectly is, to me, the second-most important proof that the greater reality being revealed to us now is altogether real.

Appendix II is a brief overview of some of the most important afterlife evidence. For a thorough and readable book on the subject, Victor and Wendy Zammit's *A Lawyer Presents the Evidence for the Afterlife* (2013) is a great summary of the best evidence. My own *The Fun of Dying – Find Out What Really Happens Next* (2010, 2014) gives you a simple explanation of how the evidence can be made to fit together, and that book includes an annotated bibliography of some seventy books listed by category. If you like, you can read for a year or two and wind up knowing as much about the afterlife as most experts have managed to learn in a lifetime.

THE GOSPELS CLINCHER

Putting aside any religious element, and putting aside even the fact that I feel called by Jesus to help Him speak to the world, the greatest discovery of my life has been the fact that after I had used the evidence to assemble a detailed view of death and the afterlife, I found that we actually have a Witness who told us two thousand years ago things about God, reality, death, the afterlife, human nature, and the meaning and purpose of human life that are precisely consistent with what we are learning now independently. Much of what Jesus says in the Gospels matches modern afterlife evidence, even in small details.

Helping you appreciate the importance of our discovery that a lot of what Jesus says in the Gospels is consistent with modern afterlife evidence is going to take us much of Chapter Four. For now, only know that the odds are long against our having in hand exactly what anybody said two thousand years ago, no matter how much that teacher was revered. So the fact that the words of Jesus in a modern English Bible are so consistent with what we are now learning from the dead seems to me to be a genuine miracle, perhaps nothing less than a revelation from God. But you be the judge of that. I only ask that you keep this point in mind as you discover in the second half of this book how consistent the afterlife evidence is with the Gospel words of Jesus.

LEARNING THE TRUTH FOR YOURSELF

As I detail in *The Fun of Dying*, and as other researchers also document, the question of what happens at and after death is no longer in dispute. We inhabit a greater reality that might be twenty times the size of this material universe, and living eternally is a natural part of every human life. If all of this is not yet clear to you, then I urge you to educate yourself! You will find it easier to understand what it is that Jesus is asking of us now if you better comprehend the greater reality in which He speaks to us. A very brief discussion of what we are learning about reality is included here as Appendix III, but beyond that I urge you to read some of the excellent books in this field. Knowledge is power! As Jesus says, **"Ask, and it will be given to you; seek, and you will find; knock, and it will** be opened to you. For everyone who asks receives, and he who seeks finds, and to him who knocks it will be opened" (MT 7:7–8).

Chapter Two
The Entire Christian Bible is Not God's Word

A major problem that all of us face in trying to understand God's truth is that in the course of choosing the books of the Christian Bible from among similar writings, those assembling the Bible decided that their choices had to be right because they were being inspired by God.

It is difficult now to imagine the level of hubris that their making this claim required! And the unfortunate result is that the religion founded in the name of Jesus is a fly in amber. It has stayed stuck in time for two millennia as the rest of the world went on. Even today, many Christians believe that the whole Christian Bible is the Inspired Word of an archaic God demanding that we also stay stuck in the first century. Until we can help Christians get past this notion, they will not hear Jesus speaking to them now.

I have read the whole Christian Bible from cover to cover a number of times. For decades, I would read a few pages each night, from Genesis through Revelation. It is this exercise of having read the Christian Bible repeatedly that makes me confident that the entire Christian Bible could not possibly be the Inspired Word of a loving and internally consistent God. Or even of a sane and rational God.

The fact that the Christian Bible doesn't hold together as a coherent unit is a problem the early Christians could have partially solved by deciding that the Gospel words of Jesus are primary. Where there is a conflict—and there are many!—the teachings of Jesus should control. But perhaps because the Inspired Word of God cannot be seen to have inconsistencies, and because the teachings of Jesus are post-legal and require a strong personal commitment, Christians have solved what should have been a big problem by making the teachings of Jesus in the Gospels no more than suggestions about how we should be living.

To most Christians, Jesus is not their Teacher. Instead, Jesus is the Lamb of God, sacrificed to redeem us from God's judgment for our sins. This easy Christian shortcut is not factual, and it is an appalling insult to God. Where on earth could it have come from?

THE COMPOSITION OF THE BIBLE

The Christian Bible consists of three parts.

The Old Testament is Jewish writings that long predate Jesus. It is good for us to have the background of the culture into which Jesus chose to be born, but the Old Testament cannot be seen to be anything more than that. It is full of outmoded cultural rules and frank barbarism. That modern Christians still read the Old Testament as the genuine God speaking to us today is a tremendous problem, as you will shortly see.

The Gospels begin the New Testament. Matthew, Mark, Luke, and John are the only books of the Bible in which the words of Jesus are reported. Given the extent to which we can corroborate the Gospel words of Jesus using modern afterlife evidence, I think it is possible to demonstrate that indeed the Gospels are God's truth being miraculously reiterated for us today.

The balance of the New Testament consists of writings of the Apostle Paul and others who were building a religion around the historical Jesus. They were first-century people using first-century understandings to build a first-century religion. Paul and the others did the best they could, and their efforts have preserved for us the Gospels' profound eternal teachings. But the balance of the New Testament is, like the Old Testament, merely an interesting cultural artifact. We can demonstrate now that it is not God's Word.

Someone said that the Old Testament and most of the New Testament are man's search for God, while the Gospels are God's search for man. And apparently now, two thousand years later, God is again attempting to reach us.

It's Turtles All the Way Down

No religion is created by God. Religions are belief systems created by people. It is reasonable to assume that each modern religion is built around core eternal teachings, just as is true of Christianity. But in every case, the people receiving those teachings built around them a religion for their own day, incorporating cultural oddities that stuck their new religion in a time capsule.

Jesus warns us about this tendency of religions to get caught up in cultural nonsense. The problem is that the cultural stuff misleads people into doing terrible things in the name of their religion. As Jesus says, **"You will know them by their fruits. Grapes are not gathered from thorn bushes nor figs from thistles, are they? So every good tree bears good fruit, but the bad tree bears bad fruit"** (MT 7:16–17).

Christians can see this problem clearly in Judaism and Islam. We love to point out all the errors of their ways. What might Jesus have to say about that?

"Why do you look at the speck that is in your brother's eye, but do not notice the log that is in your own eye? How can you say to your brother, 'Brother, let me take out the speck that is in your eye,' when you yourself do not see the log that is in your own eye? You hypocrite, first take the log out of your own eye, and then you will see clearly to take out the speck that is in your brother's eye" (LK 6:41–42).

We feel free to point out the bad fruit of all the other great religions. But as I will demonstrate to you in the next chapter, that darned log in every Christian eye keeps us from noticing that our own religion bears a bounty of terrible fruit.

Given the way that the books of the Bible were assembled by the early Church, the claim that the whole Christian Bible is the Inspired Word of God should long since have been seen as dubious. Who are we to be putting words into God's mouth? I once asked a fundamentalist friend how he could be so sure that a canon put together by committees in the equivalent of smoke-filled rooms was absolutely all inspired by God. He told me confidently that God had worked through all the participants in those councils. His answer reminded me of what had been said by a priest of a religion whose certain belief was that the world rides on the back of a turtle. When asked what the turtle was standing on, the priest had said confidently, **"It's turtles all the way down."**

In just the same way, the Christian Bible is arbitrarily and uncritically deemed by many Christians to be God's Word all the way down. This seems to me to be the fatal flaw of modern Christianity.

CHAPTER THREE
CHRISTIAN TRADITIONS DISTANCE US FROM GOD

The fact that religions are man-made belief systems built around truths that get buried in cultural traditions was a problem even in antiquity. As Jesus says, **"Why do you transgress the commandment of God for the sake of your tradition? . . . You hypocrites! Rightly did Isaiah prophesy of you: 'This people honors me with their lips, but their hearts are far away from me. But in vain do they worship me, teaching as doctrines the precepts of men'"** (MT 15:3–9).

In the same way, modern Christian traditions are of men and not of God. The confusion comes from the fact that Christians have diluted the message of Jesus by considering the Old Testament and the balance of the New Testament to be on a par with the divinely-inspired Gospels. This lack of focus on God's truth as it is revealed to us in the Gospels has stunted Christianity in peculiar ways:

1. ***No one who actually reads the Gospels can believe that Jesus means His teachings to be mere suggestions.*** By treating them as just aspirational, or even optional, Christians continue to slight the Teacher upon Whom the religion is supposed to be based.

2. ***The Christian doctrine of sacrificial redemption is not based in the teachings of Jesus, and it paints a terrible picture of God.*** Would you enjoy watching the murder of your own child? Of course not! What on earth kind of a monstrous Father would require the brutal murder of His own Son?

3. ***The Old Testament books of the Bible are full of a wrathful and often petty Jehovah God.*** Calling the Old Testament the Inspired Word of God teaches Christians to fear the genuine God. Since fear is the opposite of love, this emphasis makes it difficult for Christians to develop the intimate relationship with God that is essential to a life of spiritual growth. Christianity distances its followers from the infinite and perfect love of God. For a religion to do that is inexcusable.

4. ***The Old Testament contains a host of cultural commands that Christians do not follow.*** A lot of the Old Testament is not followed by Christians, from not wearing clothing blended of two kinds of fibers and not eating pork and separating meat from milk right through to the rules about how men can wear their hair and beards and harsh punishments for what we see as trivial infractions. And it should not be followed. These were rigid cultural rules for a harsher time thousands of years gone by. But by calling the Old Testament the Inspired Word of God and then not following parts of it, Christians are disrespecting their Deity. If it is okay to disrespect God by ignoring parts of the "divinely inspired" Old Testament, then what is to keep us from disrespecting God in other, more important ways?

5. ***Catholics and many Protestant Christians take some of the Bible's cultural rules and statements as God's Inerrant Word.*** For example, fundamentalist Christians insist that creation has to have happened in six days, that homosexuality is a grievous sin, that sexual

contact outside marriage is sinful, and that women must submit to men. Catholics historically have not allowed divorce or the use of birth control, and they have required women to cover their heads in church and priests to be celibate males. In being so adamant about enforcing these lesser and arguably outmoded cultural rules and beliefs, Christians are ignoring the warnings of Jesus against enforcing unloving rules and against judging others.

EXAMINING THE FRUIT OF THE CHRISTIAN TREE

The greatest proof that Christians are wrong in building their religion around the whole Christian Bible is that, as our beloved Teacher warns us, Christianity today bears some terrible fruit. Let's consider some lesser examples here. In Chapter Four, we'll do some poking around in the more problematic bottom of the fruit basket:

1. ***Rather than sharing the teachings of Jesus about our need to learn perfect love and forgiveness, modern Christians mostly battle for their religious traditions.*** From the fight against every form of sexual expression outside of

marriage to the insistence that only the death of Jesus on the cross can get us into heaven, Christians emphasize their religion's unloving traditions. And what may be Christianity's worst fruit of all is the self-righteous certainty so many Christians have about their own salvation and the damnation of others. Recently, a friend of mine was asked by his airplane seatmate if he knew Jesus. When my friend said that he did read Jesus and other great prophets, his seatmate sniffed, **"Oh. I just was wondering if I would see you in heaven."** And she turned away. In fighting for their misbegotten beliefs and in treating others so appallingly, many Christians give Jesus a terrible name before a world that desperately needs His teachings.

2. ***Rather than focus upon demonstrating for the world the eternal teaching of Jesus, the strictest Christians too often get caught up in self-righteous moralizing.*** My friend's airplane seatmate who smugly consigned him to hell is, regrettably, a typical Christian, as is the prominent evangelist who pulled money from a bank because it used a homosexual couple in its

advertising. He insisted that Christians must **"stop doing business with those who promote sin and stand against Almighty God's laws and His standards."** The Duggars of the TV reality show *19 Kids & Counting* insist that their children not even kiss until after they are married. When it was revealed that the oldest Duggar son had, in his early teens, sexually molested his sisters, his parents exhibited little awareness that their Old Testament attitude toward normal sexuality might have been a part of his problem. Indeed, news about the Duggars' crisis brought to light the fact that other prominent traditionalist Christians have been caught sexually molesting children. To say nothing about the Catholic Church's insistence upon celibacy for its priests, and the epidemic of priestly molestation of children that has been its fruit. In burying the eternal teachings of Jesus inside a first-century moral code that many modern people find strange and repellant, Christians continue to deny to the world the most essential set of truths that God ever has given us.

3. *Rather than concentrate on living by Jesus's Gospel teachings on love and forgiveness, many of the most devout Christians instead focus on following Old Testament customs.* For example, some very strict Christians believe that they should have as many children as possible because **"Children are a gift of the Lord, the fruit of the womb is a reward. Like arrows in the hand of a warrior, so are the children of one's youth. How blessed is the man whose quiver is full of them; they will not be ashamed when they speak with their enemies in the gate"** (Psalm 127:3–5). And then there is the appalling movement popular in some Christian circles that advocates breaking children's wills and spanking them with PVC pipe. This child abuse in the name of God comes from what seems to me to be a perverted understanding of a passage from Proverbs: **"Train up a child in the way he should go, even when he is old he will not depart from it"** (Proverbs 22:6). For modern Christians to try to live by the Old Testament's antiquated customs does nothing to spread the teachings of Jesus. Instead, it suggests to modern people that Jesus must be outmoded, too.

4. ***The Christian doctrines of original sin and sacrificial redemption erect a wall of fear between us and God.*** Christianity teaches us that we must strictly obey Old Testament rules or we risk God's judgment and eternal hellfire. Indeed, that Christian drive to instill a feeling of sinfulness in the faithful is so great that most Christian denominations teach us that no matter how we live our lives, Adam's original sin still pollutes us all. God is disgusted with us, and we had better never forget that. The adjective "God-fearing" is to Christians actually a compliment! Many Christian denominations portray God as so full of righteous rage that the only way God can forgive us simply for being who we are is by sending His only begotten Son to die horribly in our stead. That is one deeply scary God! Fear is the opposite of love: one cannot exist in the presence of the other. In teaching us from childhood that God is to be feared, Christianity puts a barrier between us and God that it can be hard for Christians ever to surmount.

5. ***The Christian doctrine of sacrificial redemption makes our greatest eternal Teacher***

into no more than a religious sacrifice. When Jesus walked the earth, first-century Jews were still sacrificing animals in their Temple. It was easy for them to imagine that the horrible death of Jesus on the cross had meant that God's Son had been delivered to sinful humankind as an act of mercy by a judgmental Jehovah God. At last we could offer a sacrifice that was great enough to get God to forgive us! The sacrifice of Jesus was such a tremendous gift from us to God that even in the twenty-first century, if we claim Him as our personal Savior, God will forgive us for being human. *Think about how absurd it is to imagine that God's putting Jesus through crucifixion might in any way have been an act of love. Such a notion made sense two thousand years ago. But why does it make sense to anybody now?* It was only after I had discovered in the course of my afterlife research that sacrificial redemption is unnecessary and it never happens that I realized how badly that Christian doctrine trivializes and humiliates Jesus. He came to us directly from God as our glorious eternal Teacher, as literally God embodied on earth. But we needn't bother to follow His teachings so long as we claim Him as our sacrifice.

CHRISTIANITY PUTS ITS TRADITIONS BEFORE THE ETERNAL WORD OF GOD

Modern Christian traditions solidify all these human-made doctrines into beliefs and practices that in every denomination are deemed to be equal to or greater than the teachings of Jesus! What might the Lord have to say about that?

"Neglecting the commandment of God, you hold to the tradition of men . . . You are experts at setting aside the commandment of God in order to keep your tradition" (MK 7:8–9).

If Jesus would not be at all happy with modern Christianity, then how would He want us to relate to God? On this point, His Gospel words are specific. It is unfortunate that so few of those who love Him follow His directions today.

"Beware of practicing your righteousness before men to be noticed by them; otherwise you have no reward with your Father who is in heaven.

"So when you give to the poor, do not sound a trumpet before you, as the hypocrites do in the

synagogues and in the streets, so that they may be honored by men. Truly I say to you, they have their reward in full. But when you give to the poor, do not let your left hand know what your right hand is doing, so that your giving will be in secret; and your Father who sees what is done in secret will reward you.

"When you pray, you are not to be like the hypocrites; for they love to stand and pray in the synagogues and on the street corners so that they may be seen by men. Truly I say to you, they have their reward in full. But you, when you pray, go into your inner room, close your door and pray to your Father who is in secret, and your Father who sees what is done in secret will reward you" (MT 6:1–6).

Christianity as it is practiced today teaches us to fear God, to minimize Jesus, to model modern life after first-century rules, and even to selectively despise our fellow man. I would argue that not only is the religion that was founded in the name of Jesus not based in the Gospel teachings of Jesus, but it bears so little relationship to what Jesus taught that unless we are willing to change it radically into what the Lord intended it to be, it is time to begin to call it something else.

I am sorry to be so blunt. I still fondly remember all the comforts of that old-time religion that for most of my life was good enough for me. But I have come to understand that for us to be comfortable in a religion that we believe gives us personal salvation while we ignore the Gospel words of Jesus that the afterlife evidence now proves to us are indeed eternal divine revelation, we betray God and we cheat our fellow man. Until Christianity reforms itself and begins to follow Jesus—and only Jesus!—we continue to delay the heaven on earth that is possible only when we live by God's truth.

CHAPTER FOUR
THE MODERN ENGLISH GOSPELS ARE GOD'S NEW REVELATION

Thomas Jefferson was an American Founding Father with an abiding interest in the Gospels. He took only the Gospels to be God's Word, and even in the Gospels he renounced such niceties as the miracles and the virgin birth. Eventually, he cut up several Bibles and pasted the words of Jesus into a copybook where he could study them in English, French, Latin, and Greek side by side, thereby creating what is known as *The Jefferson Bible*. Thomas Jefferson declared that the words of Jesus in the Bible are **"as easily distinguishable as diamonds in a dunghill,"** which sums up his attitude toward the rest of what many Christians still consider to be the Inspired Word of God. He was two hundred years ahead of his time. But were the Gospel words that Jefferson studied anything like what Jesus actually said?

The odds are long against our having now the actual words that anybody spoke two thousand years ago. I would argue, though, that what we have in the Gospels is even better than what Jesus said two thousand years ago. What we have in a modern English translation of the Gospels is what Jesus is saying TODAY.

Let's reason this through together:

1. ***Jesus is the Son of Man Who, two thousand years ago, brought the Word of God to superstitious Iron-Age folks.*** His first problem was that He had to speak to them in simple and non-threatening ways while remaining faithful to God's truth. He did that amazingly well. But we must understand that it is highly unlikely that He spoke to them back then as He would speak to us today.

2. ***When Jesus was on earth and teaching, for Him to speak against the prevailing religion was a crime punishable by death.*** Along with crowds of followers who were eager to hear His every word, Jesus was trailed by Temple guards. He had to be clever indeed if He wanted to teach important truths that went against the establishment religion while still avoiding immediate arrest. You can see even in a modern translation some of the artifices He used. Briefly:

a. His followers were constant, but the guards would change, so Jesus would deliver important truths in pieces and bits over days of time. Unless you put those different statements together, you couldn't make sense of what He actually was saying.

b. He would affirm a truth of ancient Judaism, and then he would take that truth a bit further so it was transformed from an Old Testament truth into an eternal truth. Reading the Gospels today, we have to be careful not to give undue importance to just the Old Testament parts of these statements. What is most important is the second part, the thing that Jesus really wants us to hear; and if we slight that, then we are going to misunderstand what it is that He is saying.

c. He often spoke in parables, which were simple stories that carried a more important meaning. He would tell a story and then say something like, **"He who has ears to hear, let him hear."** Wink-wink. His followers were meant to get His deeper meaning, while those ever-changing Temple guards might not.

3. ***The words of Jesus were passed down orally for decades before they were written down.*** Given that it would be surprising if His followers understood such enormous truths even as He was speaking them, it would be flat-out amazing to find that the Gospels that were first written down decades later still carried the precise words that Jesus spoke.

4. ***The words of Jesus as we have them in English have been translated twice.*** Jesus spoke Aramaic. His words were translated from Aramaic into Greek by the early Church, and from Greek they have been translated into every modern language. A few people still survive who speak the Lord's language natively, so we have recent translations of some of what Jesus said that were made directly from Aramaic into English. What is arresting, and important, is that these direct translations are much less consistent with the afterlife evidence than are the two-step translations in a modern English Bible.

5. ***The Gospels were edited by the earliest Christians as they began to build their religion.*** Not only did the formative councils report having removed some of the words of Jesus, but apparently they also wrote into the Gospels some things that they wished that Jesus had said. Fortunately, we have ways to spot the bits of coal among Thomas Jefferson's diamonds that don't fit with either the afterlife evidence or the rest of the Gospel words of Jesus, but do point toward developing Christian traditions (see Appendix I). We can assume that these were the Church councils' additions.

6. ***The Gospels have been in continuous custody of the Catholic Church for almost two thousand years.*** And for most of that time, lay-Christians were not allowed to read the Bible. While it held exclusive custody of the Gospels, the management of the Catholic Church—with the best of intentions, mind you—could have further tweaked the words of Jesus here and there.

Given all these handicaps, how are we to know that the Gospel words of Jesus in a modern English Bible can be trusted? We would love to believe that the teachings of Jesus are indeed the Inspired Word of God, but we are through with harboring the magic-thinking notion that the whole Bible, or any part of it, must be the Inspired Word of God just because someone said so. We want God's genuine truth! If only we had some independent way to verify that what Jesus says in the modern English Gospels truly is God's Word.

Well, actually, we do have such a source of validation. And it is so entirely independent of the Christian Bible that for so many correspondences to exist if the modern English Gospels are not the teachings of Jesus freshly restated for the twenty-first century is just about statistically impossible. Please read again the six points above, and suffer a moment of despair. Doesn't it make you feel distanced from Jesus to realize the course His words have had to navigate in order to survive today in any form at all, even garbled?

Now please put yourself in my shoes. I had been a devout Christian all my life, even while I spent decades studying nearly two hundred years of afterlife evidence. The evidence was so abundant and consistent, and the picture it was painting was so detailed, that when in my latter fifties I felt forced to admit that no matter how hard I looked for it, I could find no evidence that supported Christianity, I fell into a funk. By then, I had abandoned my persistent rereading of the entire Bible in favor of grazing, but I stopped at that point even looking at the Bible. I loved Jesus. I was upset to have unexpectedly proven that His religion was wrong.

And I was afraid to test Jesus. I did recall that there were some correspondences between the Gospels and what we were learning from the dead, but I had such a lifelong love for the Lord that I couldn't bear to find His mistakes. Worse, I realize now that I was in superstitious terror at having discovered that the religion that bore the name of Jesus was wrong. Could you go to hell for having learned something like that?

I remember the chill of first sitting back at my desk and staring at the wall as it sank in that I was never going to prove that Christianity was right. I had conclusive evidence that Christianity was wrong! I believe I told God right then that I was sorry. I was in such distress about what I had discovered that it took a few years for my curiosity to overcome my fears. Then one day, on what felt like a whim, I dusted off my Bible and read the Gospels in light of what I was still learning from the dead.

That was the greatest event of my life. I still recall it vividly! I read right through all four Gospels. I was nervous at first, but by Luke I was racing, heart pounding and savoring every word. Much of what Jesus says in the Gospels is supported by the afterlife evidence! He even talks about "living water." That's an odd detail that a few of the dead mention. He lays out the process of building post-death houses and coming back to bring our loved ones home and so many other things that could not be coincidental. And the nature of God, the powers of our minds, the process and the goals of spiritual growth: so much of what I had learned independently was there. I didn't yet realize how unlikely it was that we would have anything remotely near what Jesus actually had said. It was awhile before I began to think through the six points outlined above. All I knew in that moment was that Christianity might be wrong, but the Jesus that I loved was right!

Christianity is wrong, but Jesus is right. I felt alone when I first made that discovery, but I realize now as I continue to travel and speak about my death-related books that God is moving in many hearts. Surveys in western countries find that more and more people are defining themselves as less religious but more spiritual.

The field of our hearts is being cleared for fresh seeding.

MAKING SENSE OF RELIGIONS

God is eternal and unchanging, but humanity's cultural details are not. God is as central to our lives as water is to the lives of fish, and as hard for us to understand since we know no other reality. For all of human history, people have had both a superstitious terror of the unknown and a subtle awareness of the God in which they swam. Their response has been to create religions.

It is important to realize that our fear of the unknown and our desperate need to feel less helpless in a spiritual reality that we cannot comprehend is where religions come from. Indications are that our ancestors were practicing religions in ancient antiquity, perhaps from the moment when we first stood upright. We cannot place ourselves in the minds of the earliest human beings, but we can imagine how the notion of religions got started.

We know now that human minds are eternal and are inextricably part of God. Fifty thousand years ago (or even fifty years ago), this was something that nobody knew, but we were still the same eternal and spiritual beings back then that we are today. Extraordinary experiences must have been happening: signs from the dead and out-of-body experiences; communication dreams and visions. And, given what we are, that felt need for a closer connection to eternal Mind must have been ever-present. So whenever something terrible happened, the assumption that it had a supernatural agency would have made sense to those it affected. When sacrificing something to that imagined agency seemed to improve the situation, then humankind had established a relationship with a set of self-constructed deities that let us begin to feel less helpless.

Religions became fancier over the millennia. We experimented with various forms of animism and ever more sophisticated kinds of polytheism. We thought through more effective ways to placate whatever gods we had invented, and we thought through as well what awful things might happen to us if we incurred the gods' rage.

In every case, human beings and their self-constructed gods were the only ones involved in these negotiations. Never for a moment forget the fact that none of this had anything to do with the genuine, eternal God. Remember, too, that religions don't work unless we can convince ourselves that there is a spiritual actor who is able to make deals with us. Since no human-made god was real, people had to invent their gods in ways that made them seem more believable. One of the devices they used was to claim that the details of their gods had been given to them by divine revelation. So from earliest antiquity, people have been convincing themselves that religions that might seem nutty to us today were real relationships with genuine deities who had revealed themselves to humankind.

Religions continued to evolve over time. While the earliest religions seem to have assumed diffuse and manifold spiritual agency, gradually the evolution of religions tended toward fewer and more powerful gods that were less anchored to anything material.

We see the culmination of this evolution of human-made gods in the Christian Old Testament. When you read the Old Testament in that light, you will find it fascinating! The Jehovah of the Old Testament is in the mold of the ancient fear-based gods. It is not the actual God that we now know is all that exists. But it is an earnest attempt by people who craved a deeper connection to the eternal Mind of which they vaguely realized that they were a part to build the best god that they could imagine.

So, where was the genuine God while all of this was going on? We have to assume that God has always done what God continues to do today. We now know that the only thing that exists is an infinitely powerful and highly creative energy-like potentiality without size or form, alive in the sense that your mind is alive, highly emotional and therefore probably self-aware: God, in other words. Each of our minds is part of God, and everything else that we think of as real is merely an artifact of God.

Because Christianity's basis in the Old Testament's human-created Jehovah has given the genuine God a bad rap, and because each mind is part of God, some researchers refer to God as Mind, or as Source. But it really is all the same. By whichever name you prefer to use, the genuine God must always have been in communion with each individual in God's customary personae of spirit guides and angels, just as God works in our lives today.

But there was a major disconnect. While God and God's minions were caring for the Jews as they always had cared for each human being, the Jews continued to fear a cranky and judgmental Jehovah of their own making. Jehovah was not God. We understand now that God doesn't wear a human form and God has no human failings. But by the dawn of the first century of the modern era, the Jewish tribes had come to the essential threshold understanding that there is a single powerful deity. They were ready for God's first revelation. After many thousands of years, the culmination of human religious evolution was a group of monotheistic people that God might be able to wean away from their impulse to construct human-like gods so they could learn how to develop a personal relationship with the genuine God that is all that exists.

GOD REVEALS ITSELF IN JESUS

When I first understood that Jesus had not died for our sins but instead He had come to earth as our Teacher, I assumed that Jesus must have been what is called an ascended master: a very advanced human spirit, but still a regular guy. I am told that my supposition was wrong. I have been given to understand that Jesus is indeed the Son of Man, so elevated that God could "look through His eyes." As Jesus, God was born on earth in an effort to better understand how God's having given people free will could possibly have gone so wrong. In an attempt to give humankind a better start, God also meant in the person of Jesus to help the Jewish people escape the fictional construct of their religion and teach them how to relate directly to the genuine God which is all that exists.

THIS IS BIG. In the person of Jesus, God at last was revealed upon the earth. Even two thousand years and two translations later, that effort of divine revelation in the Gospels is plain to see. And it is amazing! I express no opinion of whether it ever has happened anywhere else, but it happened to the Jews two thousand years ago. We can corroborate that now.

We cannot at this point know why God's first revelation through Jesus didn't take. What seems to have happened is that the death of Jesus devastated His nascent movement. To salvage it, the Apostle Paul and others packaged up the precious teachings of Jesus in first-century Jewish beliefs and practices that were centered around their angry Jehovah and the sinfulness of Adam and the fact that in their day Jews still were sacrificing animals in their Temple. First-century people built around Jesus a first-century religion. Like every other religion before it, Christianity was built as a variation on a set of human-made and fear-based beliefs in a human-constructed deity. It was not the joyous escape from superstition and the elevation of human consciousness that God had intended.

RECOGNIZING THE WORST FRUIT OF A BAD TREE

And so two thousand years have passed. Christianity still carries the precious teachings of Jesus buried in its self-blessed scriptures, but it treats them as merely aspirational. It has ignored altogether things Jesus said that had been meant to break down that old religious artifice and teach people to relate to God individually. Jesus warns us in the Gospels against following false religions, perhaps at the time not realizing that one day He would be warning us against continuing to follow a fear-based religion that was going to be established in His name:

"Beware of the false prophets, who come to you in sheep's clothing, but inwardly are ravenous wolves. You will know them by their fruits. Grapes are not gathered from thorn bushes nor figs from thistles, are they? So every good tree bears good fruit, but the bad tree bears bad fruit. A good tree cannot produce bad fruit, nor can a bad tree produce good fruit. Every tree that does not bear good fruit is cut down and thrown into the fire. So then, you will know them by their fruits" (MT 7:15–20).

Let us look now at the very worst of Christianity's unpalatable fruit. The religion founded in the name of Jesus does not foster, and it actively impedes, the spiritual growth that both the afterlife evidence and the Gospel words of Jesus agree is the purpose of human life:

1. *It is estimated that there are now about forty thousand versions of Christianity worldwide.* Any religion that so divides what should be a people united in love is an obstacle to our spiritual growth.

2. ***Christianity does little to help us to grow spiritually.*** I was a zealous Christian for most of my life, but it was only as I studied the afterlife evidence that I came to understand what spiritual growth actually is, and why it is so important! The most common complaint I hear as I begin to talk about Christianity is that Christians don't practice what they preach. If Christianity is based in the teachings of Jesus that are meant to help us to grow spiritually, then why are there so few saintly Christians? Why are Christian old folks so little different from Christian youth in terms of their spirituality?

3. ***The Christian tradition of sacrificial redemption gives us the erroneous notion that spiritual growth requires no effort on our part.*** In many denominations, the sacrifice of Jesus on the cross can "save" us on our deathbed, no matter how we have lived our lives. It is rumored that one notable celebrity who had committed a variety of sins paid the Vatican ten million dollars to ensure that his elevator went up and not down. Good grief.

4. ***Christianity's traditions and dogmas that are not based in the teachings of Jesus obscure the importance of those teachings.*** We discover from both the afterlife evidence and the Gospels that our level of spiritual development at death will determine where we will go in the afterlife. Learning to love and forgive more perfectly is the reason why we live earth-lives, and giving us a place to develop spiritually seems to be the reason why the universe exists. Yet as best I have been able to determine, there is not one version of Christianity among all those forty thousand options that makes sharing the essential teachings of Jesus on love and forgiveness its reason for being.

5. ***Christianity teaches us to live in superstitious fear.*** The terror that Christianity induces in us is often most pronounced as death approaches, at the very time when we should be happily anticipating at last going home. Said a hospice worker quoted by Ineke Koedam in her important book, *In the Light of Death* (2014), **"Sometimes people have lived very religious lives, and this can make them rather tense on**

their deathbed . . . **I was once with a lady who was so frightened. She kept saying that she was sure she wasn't good enough to go to heaven."** A hospice volunteer said, **"I have indeed noticed that religious people who are about to die start worrying about whether or not they will be forgiven . . . I've had a whole conversation with someone about why he would go to hell, or at least not receive God's mercy."** Seeing how Christianity's fear-based traditions are polluting for some devout Christians what should be the best time of their lives breaks my heart. And it weighs heavily on Jesus.

I have listed just a few examples of the bad fruit of modern Christianity that gets in the way of our spiritual growth. I'm sure that you can think of others. These problems are built into the religion itself. They are, as Jesus says, the way that we determine what is genuinely of God and what is not.

ALLOWING GOD TO GIVE US NEW REVELATION

Apparently, Jesus has chosen the start of this new millennium to re-reveal His Gospel truths more emphatically. And this time, He is being perfectly clear about what He is doing:

1. He has ensured that we now have such abundant and consistent afterlife evidence that there is no question that the dead survive.

2. In the process of learning about the afterlife, we have come to much better understand what God is, what reality is, what we are, and the meaning and purpose of human life.

3. Jesus has made certain that the modern English translations of His Gospels are so consistent with the afterlife evidence that now we have independent validation that He knows what He is talking about.

Jesus wants us to understand that His teachings are a philosophy. How could we have had the mistaken notion that He meant to start just another religion? He speaks forcefully against religions in the Gospels. He insists that we can relate to God individually. As you listen to the Lord more carefully and realize how Christianity is ignoring His truths, you almost can see Him slapping His head in frustration.

If you are a Christian, I understand that all of this may be upsetting to you. Jesus might indeed be giving us new revelation, but how can you know that for sure? To be frank, the only way you can know it is to open your mind and let Jesus move in your heart. He is doing that for many others. He may be reaching out to you, too. You mustn't take my word for anything! But I do hope that you will listen to the Lord.

If you believe that Jesus died for your sins, then for Him to request that in return you open your mind and really listen to His words doesn't seem to be a lot to ask.

What Jesus is Saying to Us Today

Chapter Five
Jesus Wants Us to Know the Genuine God

Here are two pieces of irony!

- Religions do not improve our relationship with God. Instead, they get in the way of it.

- Jesus in the Gospels strongly suggests that we learn to get past religions. Instead of doing that, we have used the religion that was established in His name to maintain a fear-based separation between us and God for another two thousand years.

That we think of religions and God as inextricably tight is a cultural artifact. Since ancient prehistory, people have been inventing gods and encasing them in religions as a way to cope with superstitious fears of so many things they had no way to understand. Religions are man-made. Many of them profess to having been established by a god or gods, but we have learned in the course of studying the afterlife that there is just one genuine God. And that God is not related to any religion.

THE GREATEST SCIENTIFIC BREAKTHROUGH OF ALL TIME

Before the early twentieth century, science was theoretically an open-minded search for the truth. But then, about a hundred years ago, teams of the dead began to deliver astonishing and incontrovertible proofs that they were happily still alive. To forestall having to consider these amazing new afterlife communications, university departments and scientific journals began to enforce what they then called the "fundamental scientific dogma" of materialism. This made life easier for them, but over time it has contorted most scientific disciplines into knots. Consumer technology has been little affected, and scientists still put up a brave front, but when you read popular science magazines you can see them desperately shoving fingers and fists into ever more of the places where their materialist dike is crumbling. Oh no! The cosmological constants are not constant! More than ninety-five percent of the universe is non-material! Subatomic particles turn out to be just vortices of energy, so can we still call them particles? How can eighty percent of the light in the nearby universe be non-material? What the heck is going on?

It is a sad testimony to the stymied state of affairs in modern scientific inquiry that today some of the biggest discoveries are being made by afterlife researchers. We began by simply trying to figure out what happens at and after death, but what we have found as we tugged harder on that string is a whole new science, a third wave of physics, a fresh understanding of reality that within decades will altogether transform the world.

What we think of as consciousness is all that exists. This discovery arises naturally from the quantum mechanics that was first gaining prominence early in the last century, at about the time when teams of the dead were delivering astounding proofs of their survival. I even suspect that the simultaneous timing of these two developments was deliberate. We understand now that many scientific breakthroughs originate in the afterlife levels and are channeled to the minds of earthly researchers. It is not a stretch to imagine that as the earliest quantum physicists were being assisted in achieving their insights, those teams of dead researchers were attempting to supplement the physicists' work with spectacular proofs that human minds are powerful and eternal.

In a world of honest scientific inquiry, each of these advances could have enhanced the other. As it was, the mainstream scientific reaction to published volumes of the results of book-tests and other survival proofs was to flat refuse for the foreseeable future to consider investigating any evidence that might hint at an intelligence underlying reality. Fortunately, even without the corroborating testimony of those teams of the dead, the pioneering quantum physicists seem to have understood what it was that they had found.

Max Planck won the 1918 Nobel Prize in physics as the father of quantum mechanics. In 1931, Planck said, **"I regard consciousness as fundamental. I regard matter as derivative from consciousness. We cannot get behind consciousness. Everything that we talk about, everything that we regard as existing, postulates consciousness."** By 1944, he was positing a force that controls the atom. He said, **"We must assume behind this force the existence of a conscious and intelligent mind. This mind is the matrix of all matter."**

Eureka! Max Planck had discovered God as scientific fact. Mainstream physicists couldn't explore this insight without risking their careers in materialist science, but afterlife researchers have seized on Planck's work as a breathtaking way to make better sense of what the dead have long been telling us.

WHAT WE NOW UNDERSTAND IS TRUE ABOUT GOD

Jesus doesn't tell us a lot about God. He refers to God as "Father" or "Heavenly Father," and He makes it clear that God as Spirit is within us, but that is about it. The Gospels leave us hungry to know more, but Jesus is speaking to simple people and He can't risk speaking against the prevailing religion so He doesn't go into much detail. Fortunately, those we used to think were dead do not share the Lord's constraints.

Modern afterlife evidence is full of insights into the eternal God that is the only thing that is real. These insights are consistent with what Jesus says, and very consistent across reports from the dead. If Jesus were speaking to us today, this is likely what He would tell us about God:

Every Human Mind is Part of God. There is no separation between you and God, and no separation between you and other people. There is one eternal Consciousness.

God is Love. Christians say this, but the religion is so full of superstitions and dogmas and tensions among Christian denominations that it is hard to fathom what the Christian version of the word "love" even means. Thanks to our new revelation from Jesus that the love that He teaches is God's only law, we can sweep all that Christian confusion aside and for the first time truly grasp the fact that God is love beyond our ability to fathom it. God is as emotional as we are emotional, but God does not know any emotion except for intense and perfect love.

God is Good. Having lived for so long in a Christian reality in which the notion of a devil is strong, for a long time I wondered how much evil exists and how much of a threat it is to us. Well, the afterlife evidence demonstrates that in reality, the good guys have the power. What evil exists is pitifully small when compared with the infinite power of God, and I am embarrassed to note that a lot of the evil that exists was created by human beings. Absent the annoying mosquito-effect of a bit of negativity here and there, this universe and all of reality are gentler and more profoundly supportive than we on this tough planet can imagine.

God is Power. In the consciousness-based physics that governs nearly all of reality, and even in this material five percent or so of reality where a clumsier subset of physics holds sway, what we think of as spiritual perfection is the source of every power. Your Daddy is the toughest Dude on the universal playground! We can demonstrate that conclusively now. Just stick with the genuine God, and nothing whatsoever can harm you.

God is Light. Beyond this material universe—that is, in most of reality—there are no suns. Instead, most of the dimensions of reality are lit by God and by God alone, so the lower vibratory dimensions, those farthest from the Source, are dark; while the higher dimensions are brighter and brighter the closer they come to God's vibratory center. Beyond materiality, Consciousness is light. Each "I," each speck of consciousness, also appears beyond materiality to be light, with the more advanced specks of course much brighter. Those who have died tell us that the wonderful white light that fills the Summerland levels of the afterlife feels like being bathed in God's love.

God is Spirit. There are some reports in near-death experiences of people actually seeing God, but the dead tell us that the genuine God never takes corporeal form. We know that those who have near-death experiences don't visit the places where the dead reside, and we also know that much of what they experience is pulled from their own beliefs because they will be going back and their spirit guides don't want to confuse them. This is why very religious people will have NDEs full of aberrant religious symbols. But the fact that we are repeatedly assured that God never takes human form makes more remarkable the new information that Jesus actually did embody God, both for God's edification and to make a valiant effort to reveal to primitive and superstitious people God's eternal truth. The more you learn, the more you realize that God's love for us is limitless. God's patience with us defies our understanding.

God is our Source and our Destination. As best we can puzzle it out from the evidence, each bit of consciousness—each "I," if you will—experiences the illusion of separation from God but without ever actually leaving God, and then immediately each of us is striving to return to our Source. These are human concepts which of course aren't right, but they are somewhat analogous to what the evidence suggests is happening. We are in materiality to better grow spiritually. Once our growth is perfected, we gladly graduate back to God.

God Doesn't Care About Religions. We have found no evidence whatsoever that God cares one whit whether you are religious. Religions are man-made superstitions fed by human fears of the unknown and by our subconscious drive to return to God. And there is evidence that each earth-religion has an after-death haven for its adherents that is mind-created by co-religionists. So not only do you not have to be religious to get into heaven, but to be a closed-minded follower of one of the more extreme sects of any religion will just buy you an unnecessary after-death stay in an off-track limbo of religionism.

God Helps Itself. Since everything is God, it is erroneous to think of God and angels and spirit guides and you and me as separate beings. There is overwhelming evidence that each of us on earth is surrounded by non-material helpers, spirit guides and angels, each of whom is also an "I." Each "I," whether or not it is currently in a body, is working toward its own spiritual perfection, and a big part of that work is helping others. Each of us is not just IN God's hands, but we ARE God's hands. God is all there is.

God Creates With and Through Us. On earth, we are bound by the laws of a Mind-created, mathematics-based physics that is designed to keep our minds from messing with this material universe. Still, there is evidence that even here the most spiritually advanced of us can affect matter with our minds. And since we are of the same consciousness as God, beyond this universe many of us are able to create what appear to be new realities as solid-seeming as the earth but more gorgeous, like earth-perfection magnified. There are wonderful earthlike Summerland levels to which we go immediately after our bodies die, places full of flowers in incredible colors and magnificent buildings of every description, and the evidence suggests that all of this is mind-created over eons by earth-graduates. Husbands replicate favorite earth-homes for their later-arriving wives. Scientists create laboratories so newly-arrived colleagues can continue their research in a place where they can have better access to information, and from which whatever they develop can be channeled to living scientists when the time is right. (Appendix III is a very brief summary of what we have learned about the afterlife.)

God Is All That Exists. Think about that, really think about it, and you change your life forever. It is easy to say that you and everyone you know and everything you see, whether animate or inanimate, is God and nothing but God. The evidence indicates that this is true; say it, and the words roll off your tongue. But stop and think about what that means!

DEVELOPING A RELATIONSHIP WITH THE GENUINE GOD

If you have a religion-based view of God, you will need to get rid of as much of that as possible before you can begin to enjoy the intimacy with God that is your birthright. Apparently, God has patiently waited for us to mature sufficiently that we might get past that religious crutch. Our transition to a genuine relationship with God was supposed to have begun two thousand years ago. It is Jesus's hope that it will at last begin now.

Jesus makes it clear in the Gospels that practicing a religion gets in the way of our ability to draw close to God. But why must that be? Why have so few religious people achieved the heightened awareness of God that is essential to a life of spiritual growth? Jesus nails one of the reasons why. Most religious folks get so wound up in the traditions of their religions that they settle for form and forget that seeking a closer relationship with God is the reason why they are practicing a religion in the first place.

"And why do you yourselves transgress the commandment of God for the sake of your tradition? . . . You hypocrites, rightly did Isaiah prophesy of you: 'This people honors me with their lips, but their heart is far

away from me. But in vain do they worship me, teaching as doctrines the precepts of men'" (MT 15:3–9).

Another problem with religions, of course, is that they are human institutions. As such, they provide an opportunity for some people to seize control over others. There is so much power and money potentially inherent in being a religious leader that clergymen have a strong motivation to keep their flocks fearfully subservient. Jesus was wise to this problem when He last was on earth:

"Beware of the scribes who like to walk around in long robes, and like respectful greetings in the market places, and chief seats in the synagogues and places of honor at banquets, who devour widows' houses, and for appearance's sake offer long prayers; these will receive greater condemnation" (MK 12:38–40). The word "scribe" here is in some Bible versions translated as "teacher of the law." **"Woe to you religious lawyers! For you have taken away the key of knowledge; you yourselves did not enter, and you hindered those who were entering"** (LK 11:52). **"But woe to you, scribes and Pharisees, hypocrites, because you shut off the kingdom of heaven from people; for you do not enter in yourselves, nor do you allow those who are entering to go in"** (MT 23:13).

I wince for modern-day Christian clergy still preaching unloving Old Testament rules whenever I read the Lord's condemnations of the clergy of his day who enforced religious laws but did not teach people how to develop spiritually. First-century scribes and religious lawyers didn't have the teachings of Jesus to guide them, but that excuse is not available to modern Christian clergymen. Every Bible they thump still carries within it the Gospel teachings of Jesus that we now know, based upon the afterlife evidence, are the truest and most complete prescription for spiritual growth that God ever has given to us.

"But go and learn what this means: 'I desire mercy, not sacrifice.' For I have not come to call the righteous, but sinners" (MT 9:13). **"Truly, truly, I say to you, if anyone keeps My word he will never see death"** (JN 8:51).

Instead of feeling bound by the traditions of any religion, Jesus urges us to begin to relate to God on our own. **"But you, when you pray, go into your inner room, close your door and pray to your Father who is in secret, and your Father who sees what is done in secret will reward you"** (MT 6:6).

LIBERATING JESUS FROM CHRISTIANITY

The primary reason why our relationship with God must be established individually is one that we will explore in the next chapter. But first, it is important for anyone who might be harboring the lingering thought that Jesus wants to be a religious figure to consider some facts:

1. ***The primary traditions of Christianity do not come from Jesus in the Gospels.*** Instead, they come from the rest of the Bible. They have nothing to do with God's eternal truths as Jesus taught them.

2. ***Every hint in the Gospels that Jesus might have had the establishment of a religion in mind can be shown to be a later edit.*** See Appendix I for a discussion of the Gospels' red-letter words that we can demonstrate did not come from Jesus.

3. ***Jesus tried during His lifetime to squelch the religion that His followers were building around Him.*** He insisted that instead they focus on His words. You can feel the Lord's swelling frustration as He sputters, **"Why do you call me 'Lord, Lord,' and do not do what I say?"** (LK 6:46). **"Not everyone who says to me, 'Lord, Lord,' will enter the kingdom of heaven, but only he who does the will of my Father who is in heaven will enter"** (MT 7:21). Patiently, he

keeps on making it clear that, **"If you continue in My word, then you are truly disciples of Mine; and you will know the truth, and the truth will make you free"** (JN 8:31–32).

4. *Jesus warned his followers that trying to merge His new philosophy with Judaism would make a mess and would ruin them both.* Of course, this is just what eventually was done. Here is further confirmation that the religion-building was beginning while Jesus was still on earth. **"But no one puts a patch of unshrunk cloth on an old garment; for the patch pulls away from the garment, and a worse tear results. Nor do people put new wine into old wineskins; otherwise the wineskins burst, and the wine pours out and the wineskins are ruined; but they put new wine into fresh wineskins, and both are preserved"** (MT 9:16–17).

5. *Jesus tried to help His followers find ways to keep His teachings separate from Judaism.* He urged clergymen to become disciples of His new philosophy of love and forgiveness, suggesting that they would be able to do that while they still

remained in their old religion. **"Therefore every scribe who has become a disciple of the kingdom of heaven is like a head of a household, who brings out of his treasure things new and old"** (MT 13:52).

Over and over, Jesus urges us to listen to His words and use them to build our best and most spiritually productive lives. For you to be a professed Christian is not enough for the Lord! He actually does expect you to follow His teachings perfectly. **"Therefore everyone who hears these words of Mine and acts on them may be compared to a wise man who built his house on the rock. And the rain fell, and the floods came, and the winds blew and slammed against that house; and yet it did not fall, for it had been founded on the rock. Everyone who hears these words of Mine and does not act on them, will be like a foolish man who built his house on the sand. The rain fell, and the floods came, and the winds blew and slammed against that house; and it fell—and great was its fall"** (MT 7:24–27).

But still, Jesus seems to have realized that those seeking to make His teachings the core of a new variant of Judaism were going to have their way. He made sure to urge us to look behind whatever religion might purport to speak for Him, and always to come back to Him directly. He is our ultimate source of God's truth. Today and eternally He says, **"So I say to you, ask, and it will be given to you; seek, and you will find; knock, and it will be opened to you. For everyone who asks, receives; and he who seeks, finds; and to him who knocks, it will be opened"** (LK 11:9–10).

Chapter Six
The Kingdom of God is Within You

It is impossible for anything to bring you closer to the genuine God than you already are. The greatest scientific discovery in history was best expressed by Max Planck nearly a century ago, although other physicists have grasped it as well because the modern insight that human consciousness is primary and must pre-exist matter is a bastard child of quantum mechanics. Max Planck won the 1918 Nobel Prize as the father of quantum theory. And his discovery that human consciousness is primary and pre-existing led Planck inexorably to the scientific discovery of the genuine God. Even today, mainstream physicists grumpily dispute that this is what their hero meant to say, but it is clear that Planck realized what he had found.

He said in 1944, **"As a man who has devoted his whole life to the most clear headed science, to the study of matter, I can tell you as a result of my research about atoms this much: There is no matter as such. All matter originates and exists only by virtue of a force which** brings the particle of an atom to vibration and holds this most minute solar system of the atom together. We must assume behind this force the existence of a conscious and intelligent mind. This mind is the matrix of all matter."

Simply capitalize "Force" and "Mind" and you arrive at an intellectual singularity, the place where God and science meet.

BEGINNING TO FIND GOD WITHIN OURSELVES

We know now, based upon abundant evidence, that each human mind is inextricably part of eternal Mind. Jesus said the same thing two thousand years ago, but He said it in ways that simple people might understand. He said, **"The kingdom of God is not coming with signs to be observed; nor will they say, 'Look, here it is!' or, 'There it is!' For behold, the kingdom of God is in your midst"** (LK 17:20–21). Some translations say **"the Kingdom of God is within you."** Jesus also said, **"God is spirit, and those who worship Him must worship in spirit and in truth"** (JN 4:24). **"It is the Spirit who gives life; the flesh profits nothing; the words that I have spoken to you are spirit and are life"** (JN 6:63).

Jesus refers often to the Kingdom of Heaven and the Kingdom of God. When you read His Gospels closely, you conclude that these terms denote a state of advanced spiritual development that might correspond in the afterlife to Level Six and above (see also Chapter 9 and Appendix III). Working toward such exalted spiritual growth is the purpose of each human life. For all of humankind to achieve that level of spiritual development, to the point where it takes over all the earth, is what we pray for in the Lord's Prayer when we say, **"Your kingdom come. Your will be done, on earth as it is in heaven"** (MT 6:10). Jesus tells us in the Gospels that elevating the consciousness of the planet to this extent is OUR job. It never was His! Jesus did His part two thousand years ago by sharing with us His precise prescription for bringing God's Kingdom to all the earth. And only by carefully following His teachings do we have a prayer of making it happen.

There came a sunny afternoon when the Temple guards were especially attentive so Jesus had to speak more obscurely as He urged His followers to stop thinking of God as a very large human with a beard. He said, **"If you love me, you will keep my commandments. I will ask the Father, and He will give you another Helper, that He may be with you forever; that is the Spirit of truth, whom the world cannot receive, because it does not see Him or know Him, but you know Him because He abides with you and will be in you"** (JN 14:15–17).

The Kingdom Of God Is Within You

This is a pretty succinct explanation of the fact that God is indwelling Spirit, only tweaked a bit so Jesus could escape arrest for speaking against the prevailing religion. Those who later were in the process of establishing Christianity ignored the part about following the teachings of Jesus, but instead they fixed on the odd detail that apparently God was somehow doubled. Or, no, God was tripled! Jesus must be an aspect of God as well. From this misunderstanding of Jesus's attempt to tell His followers that God is Spirit while He fooled the Temple guards for one more day came the odd, polytheistic notion that the Christian God is three-in-one. There is no evidence for a Trinity, just as there is no evidence for sacrificial redemption. So we can freshly read these words of Jesus as another creative attempt to tell us that God is indwelling Spirit, and to insist that since this is the case, we don't need to follow any religion. All we need to do is to open our hearts to the God of which each of us is a part, and to follow the Lord's teachings as He leads us toward ever more rapid spiritual growth.

68

OUR MINDS ARE POWERFULLY PART OF AN INFINITELY POWERFUL GOD

Christian traditions ignore something that strikes a modern nonreligious reader. Jesus in the Gospels says a lot about the power of our minds to affect reality:

"Daughter, take courage; your faith has made you well" (MT 9:22).

(Healing a blind man) **"Do you believe that I am able to do this?" . . . It shall be done to you according to your faith"** (MT 9:28–29).

(When Peter couldn't walk on water) **"You of little faith, why did you doubt?"** (MT 14:31).

"Jesus said, **'Someone did touch Me, for I was aware that power had gone out of Me.'** When the woman saw that she had not escaped notice, she came trembling and fell down before Him, and declared in the presence of all the people the reason why she had touched Him, and how she had been immediately healed. And He said to her, **'Daughter, your faith has made you well; go in peace'"** (LK 8:46–48).

"Have faith in God. Truly I say to you, whoever says to this mountain, 'Be taken up and cast into the sea,' and does not doubt in his heart, but believes that what he says is going to happen, it will be granted him.

Therefore I say to you, all things for which you pray and ask, believe that you have received them, and they will be granted you" (MK 11:22–24).

It was this repeated insistence by Jesus on the God-like power of our minds that first made me know the magnitude of my discovery that what Jesus tells us in the Gospels is genuinely the Word of God. There I sat on my brave and climactic afternoon, uneasily reading red-letter sentence after red-letter sentence, still in superstitious terror because proving that Christianity was wrong might be something that I could live with, but discovering that Jesus had not been right would be a calamity beyond bearing.

I was seeing some encouraging signs. I hadn't yet found any real bloopers. Then I read that well-known passage about telling a mountain to throw itself into the sea, and for the first time I understood what Jesus was saying. He was telling us that once we really believe in the power of our own minds to affect matter, that power is within us, so even moving a mountain is not beyond our grasp.

Look around you. Understand that your own mind is part of the infinitely powerful eternal Mind that continuously manifests everything that you see.

Even your own individual mind is much greater than you can imagine! It is in the nature of our earth-experience that we have little access to most of our minds while we are in these bodies. We have accepted a voluntary amnesia as part of the deal that we make in entering earth-lives, and the material brain further limits what our awareness can access. Most of your mind is what scientists call your subconscious mind, but we afterlife researchers call it by a more accurate title: it is your superconscious mind, or perhaps your oversoul. The dead tell us that soon after death, our earth-awareness merges with our superconscious mind, and suddenly we have access to memories and understanding and much greater power.

Read the above paragraph again. Now realize on a deeper level that this earth-lifetime will be over in a moment. And the bodily death that used to seem sad will instead be for you a joyous return to home because an integral part of the infinitely powerful and all-loving God is who you always will be.

CHAPTER SEVEN
LOVE IS GOD'S ONLY LAW

Jesus replaces all Ten Commandments and every other Old Testament rule with just one commandment: that we love perfectly. Actually, God's commandment that we love is so essential to our spiritual growth that Jesus gives it to us in two ways. For those who are not caught up in first-century Christian rules and dogmas, He simply says:

"A new commandment I give to you, that you love one another, even as I have loved you, that you also love one another" (JN 13:34).

If you are an adherent of any religion other than Christianity, or if you have no religion at all, then this is all you'll need in order to grasp the universal philosophy of Jesus! His is a powerful way of thinking that will enable you to achieve undreamed-of spiritual growth and enjoy your best life both now and forevermore.

If you are a Christian, on the other hand, you are encumbered by all that Old Testament legalism that you were reared to believe is the Inspired Word of God. So where does love fit in for you? Jesus has a two-step answer.

Someone asked Him one day whether what He was doing with these new teachings was really just abolishing the Law and the Prophets, which was what the Jews of His day called the Christian Old Testament. With one eye on the listening Temple guards, Jesus said, **"Do not think that I came to abolish the Law or the Prophets; I did not come to abolish but to fulfill"** (MT 5:17).

What did Jesus mean by that? Different day, different guards, someone asked Him what was the greatest commandment. Jesus said, **"'You shall love the Lord your God with all your heart, and with all your soul, and with all your mind.' This is the great and foremost commandment. The second is like it, 'You shall love your neighbor as yourself.' On these two commandments depend the whole Law and the Prophets"** (MT 22:37–40).

Do you see what Jesus is doing here? He is saying that when He said earlier that He had come to fulfill the Old Testament, what He meant was that now that we have His teachings, we don't need religious rules anymore. He is taking all the Law and the Prophets—the entire Old Testament, including all Ten Commandments—and replacing it with the beautiful new directive that we must love God and love one another. He also gives it to us from another perspective, affirming that the Golden Rule sums up the entire Old Testament:

"In everything, therefore, treat people the same way you want them to treat you, for this is the Law and the Prophets" (MT 7:12).

Pardon me for shouting, but here is the most important thing that I ever will write:

THE TRUTH THAT LOVE IS GOD'S ONLY LAW IS ETERNAL DIVINE REVELATION, FIRST GIVEN TWO THOUSAND YEARS AGO AND MIRACULOUSLY RESTATED FOR US TODAY.

I wish I could write that in the sky above you! Once you really internalize and begin to live by God's command that we love, in all things and in every moment, you will make worthwhile the Lord's whole effort in coming to earth, in suffering, in dying, in patiently watching for two thousand years, and then in feeling the need to reveal His truth again to us now. We have at last advanced to the point where we can dispense with religious rules and learn to live our lives governed by love! And finally, two thousand years after Jesus first revealed that love is God's only law, we can now begin our beautiful task of sharing the Lord's teachings with all the world and building the Kingdom of God on earth.

It seems that even in the time of Jesus, leading Jews were coming to understand that the entire Old Testament could be boiled down to simply the commands that we love God and love our neighbor. I find it fascinating that an expert in Jewish law would give Jesus the answer that he does here, although of course this could be a later edit. Let this familiar parable speak to you anew:

"And a lawyer stood up and put Him to the test, saying, **'Teacher, what shall I do to inherit eternal life?'**

"And He said to him, **'What is written in the Law? How does it read to you?'**

"And he answered, **'You shall love the Lord your God with all your heart, and with all your soul, and with all your strength, and with all your mind; and your neighbor as yourself.'**

"And He said to him, **'You have answered correctly; do this and you will live.'**

"But wishing to justify himself, he said to Jesus, **'And who is my neighbor?'**

"Jesus replied and said, **'A man was going down from Jerusalem to Jericho, and fell among robbers, and they stripped him and beat him, and went away leaving him half dead. And by chance a priest was going down on that road, and when he saw him, he passed by on the other side. Likewise a Levite also, when he came to the** place and saw him, passed by on the other side. But a Samaritan, who was on a journey, came upon him; and when he saw him, he felt compassion, and came to him and bandaged up his wounds, pouring oil and wine on them; and he put him on his own beast, and brought him to an inn and took care of him. On the next day he took out two denarii and gave them to the innkeeper and said, "Take care of him; and whatever more you spend, when I return I will repay you." Which of these three do you think proved to be a neighbor to the man who fell into the robbers' hands?'

"And he said, **'The one who showed mercy toward him.'**

"Then Jesus said to him, **'Go and do the same'**" (LK 10:25–37).

Now, the priest and the Levite were Jewish clergymen. The Samaritan was a member of a denigrated religious sect. In addition to this simple illustration of what would be the loving thing to do, Jesus may be emphasizing for us the fact that religious status and affiliations don't matter. What is important to our spiritual health is how well we give our love to others.

JESUS CAME TO US AS OUR TEACHER

Jesus refers to Himself in the Gospels as the Son of Man, a term whose meaning is unclear, although He may simply be referring to the fact that He is an elevated being born into a human body. If indeed God were indwelling in that body in order to experience the human state, as the dead now suggest to us was true, then "Son of Man" may have been God's own term. Jesus refers to Himself as the Son of Man, but those around Him commonly call him the Teacher, and it is on His teachings that His own emphasis is placed. Repeatedly He says some version of, **"Truly, truly, I say to you, if anyone keeps my word he will never see death"** (JN 8:51).

Jesus's teachings amount to the sole command that we learn to love perfectly. What He says is devoid of rules; it is essentially post-legal. He refers to sin frequently, but He seems in most places where the word turns up to be talking about not the breaking of laws, but rather a spiritual falling-short. For example, He says, **"And whoever receives one such child in My name receives Me; but whoever causes one of these little ones who believe in Me to stumble, it would be better for him to have a heavy millstone hung around his neck, and to be drowned in the depth of the** sea" (MT 18:5–6). The word "stumble" here is in some Bible versions translated as "sin."

Jesus's command that we love perfectly got buried as the Christian Bible was put together. If everything is the Inspired Word of God, then nothing can stand out as more important. And when you've got Old Testament behavioral rules that Jehovah is insisting that you follow, a soft command that you love (whatever the word "love" might mean here) does not stand much of a chance. Worse, Christianity promptly gave Jesus the alternate role of being sacrificed to redeem us from God's judgment, so then whatever He had said in the Gospels was seen to be ancillary to His primary purpose.

No one who actually reads the Gospels without the encumbrance of Christian traditions can believe that Jesus's command that we love perfectly is meant to be just a suggestion. He reiterates it repeatedly! He says, **"But love your enemies, and do good, and lend, expecting nothing in return; and your reward will be great, and you will be sons of the Most High; for He Himself is kind to ungrateful and evil men. Be merciful, just as your Father is merciful"** (LK 6:35–36). **"You have heard that it was said, 'You shall love your neighbor and hate your enemy.' But I say to you, love your enemies and pray for those who persecute you, so that you may be sons of**

your Father who is in heaven . . . you are to be perfect, as your heavenly Father is perfect" (MT 5:43–48).

The role of sacrifice that Christianity assigns to Jesus is bogus. God already perfectly loves and forgives us. And Jesus came to us as our Teacher! When He walked the earth, He was altogether focused on His need to teach us how to love more perfectly as our gateway to spiritual growth.

"You are to be perfect, as your heavenly Father is perfect" (MT 5:48). The dead agree with Jesus that in fact this is the standard. "Close enough" might work in pitching horseshoes, but when each of us has our post-death life review, we will feel the emotions of all the people we affected during our entire lives. We will agonize over little things, the disappointments we caused, the feelings we hurt, and every time that we acted selfishly.

Those who have lived their lives as Christians have been known to express their post-death shock that the standard for the way we live our lives is a lot higher than they had been told. And the legalism of "sin" is only in our minds, since God never judges anyone. I have seen no evidence that God cares whether we obey even one Old Testament law. But after our deaths, we are going to care very much about each time in our life review when we catch ourselves doing something that is even a little bit unloving. (We discuss the life-review process in Chapter 8.)

LOVE IS CRUCIALLY IMPORTANT

We are so used to religious legalisms that the thought of boiling down every religious rule to just the command that we love God and also love one another might strike us as simplistic. Why love, in particular? We are accustomed in our culture to thinking of love as something like emotional candy, a grace note in life but not central to it. Why does God even care whether we love anyone?

This is the sort of fundamental question that we cannot yet fully answer, but two related explanations come to mind:

1. *Love seems to be the way in which we feel and express the primary law of spiritual physics.* In a greater reality governed by consciousness that might be twenty times the size of the material universe, it turns out that love, or what we might call consciousness's affinity for itself, is what determines the vibratory rate of our minds, and therefore the highest afterlife level that we can attain. In a reality that is consciousness-based, emotion is a physical force. The most positive

81

emotion that exists is love, and as such it is the ultimate source of all power.

2. ***Love is a vast improvement over legalisms.***
   Religious laws are clumsy. They don't allow for value judgments or motives or mercy. They are meant to induce in us the behaviors that would flow from spiritual growth without helping us to attain that growth. And what may be worse, it is much too easy for people to use religious laws to judge and condemn one another. Legalisms do little to help us grow spiritually, while learning more perfect love turns out to be the very essence of spiritual growth.

What does Jesus mean by "love"? It is important to note that He puts the love of God first. Until you have an open and entirely loving relationship with God, I don't think that you even can see other people as you must see them in order to love them. Your intimate relationship with your Source is the essential core of your spiritual life.

Indeed, your intimate relationship with God is the most important part of every aspect of your life! And once you have well established it, you will find that every care is gone. Jesus says, **"For this reason I say to you, do not be worried about your life, as to what you will eat or what** you will drink; nor for your body, as to what you will put on. Is not life more than food, and the body more than clothing? Look at the birds of the air, that they do not sow, nor reap nor gather into barns, and yet your heavenly Father feeds them. Are you not worth much more than they?

"And who of you by being worried can add a single hour to his life? And why are you worried about clothing? Observe how the lilies of the field grow; they do not toil nor do they spin, yet I say to you that not even Solomon in all his glory clothed himself like one of these. But if God so clothes the grass of the field, which is alive today and tomorrow is thrown into the furnace, will He not much more clothe you? You of little faith! Do not worry then, saying, 'What will we eat?' or 'What will we drink?' or 'What will we wear for clothing?' For the Gentiles eagerly seek all these things; for your heavenly Father knows that you need all these things. But seek first His kingdom and His righteousness, and all these things will be added to you" (MT 6:25–33).

It was my new need to learn to love God perfectly that brought me to the point where I could no longer be a practicing Christian. While I was still in the religion, I was too fearful to love God as each of us needs to love God in order to really grow spiritually. If, like me, you have a religion-derived notion of God that makes you fearful, then you also are likely to find that you cannot properly love God until you are free to love God. We must love God without reservation as Father and Source, and even as an aspect of ourselves. As Jesus tells us, the kingdom of God is within us.

Freeing yourself from religious fears is not as difficult as you might think. Simply trust in God and claim your freedom! Thank God every day for the fact that God's love for you is perfect and you have nothing whatsoever to fear. As you begin to believe what you are saying, your fears should start to dissipate like mist. Perhaps in part because Christianity has instilled in us so many fears surrounding death, it can help a lot for you to learn as much as possible about what actually happens at death. Fear of death is the base fear, and as you begin to learn what is true about death, you will altogether lose your fear of it. When Jesus says **"you will know the truth, and the truth will set you free,"** (JN 8:32) He is speaking profoundest wisdom.

LEARNING TO LOVE OTHER PEOPLE

So we must begin by learning to love God, completely and free from superstitious fears. How then should we love other people? Jesus gives us a remarkable clue in one of His quotations above that I'll bet you didn't catch. He says, **"Love your neighbor as yourself"** (MT 22:39). Most Christians read this as if Jesus is saying, "Love your neighbor as if he were yourself," but in every translation of those words I have seen, the "as if he were" is absent. It was only after I had done considerable afterlife research and come to realize that our minds are not only made in God's likeness, but actually are part of God, that I realized why Jesus puts it that way.

You and your neighbor are one being. Your neighbor truly IS yourself. Everyone you see on the street is a part of you. Every ex with whom you are at lifelong war, every African dying of starvation, every terrorist, and every saint: all are inextricably part of you. Everyone. There are no exceptions. I have found understanding this core fact about my relationship with other people to be a decent start at trying to figure out how God wants us to love our neighbor.

Jesus does give us further clues about what loving other people means to Him. All of what He says about love is full of the emotion of a Man on a mission. When taken together, His words paint a compelling picture.

"While He was still speaking to the crowds, behold, His mother and brothers were standing outside, seeking to speak to Him. Someone said to Him, **'Behold, Your mother and Your brothers are standing outside seeking to speak to You.'** But Jesus answered the one who was telling Him and said, **'Who is My mother and who are My brothers?'** And stretching out His hand toward His disciples, He said, **'Behold My mother and My brothers! For whoever does the will of My Father who is in heaven, he is My brother and sister and mother'''** (MT 12:46–50).

Now, putting aside my crankiness that Jesus was slighting His own mother, what I take from this passage is an insistence on His part that everyone is alike in His affection. He is asking us to take the kind of love that we have for those closest to us, and spread that love to all the world.

As I will explain further in Appendix I, not everything that Jesus is reported in the Gospels to have said is supported by the afterlife evidence, and nor is it even consistent with the remainder of His Gospel words. Where something that Jesus is reported in the Gospels to have said is (a) at variance with the afterlife evidence; (b) inconsistent with other of His Gospel words; and, importantly, (c) just what those who were establishing Christian dogmas would have been eager to find Jesus saying in the Gospels, then we have discovered a bit of coal hidden among what Thomas Jefferson called the diamonds that are the words of Jesus. Not only are we entitled to pluck out these bits of coal, but we are compelled to get rid of them. It is impossible while the coal remains to really understand what Jesus is saying.

Thus we find what is a beautiful and profound teaching about loving our neighbor that is unfortunately encased in a shell of coal. Jesus is quoted as saying:

"But when the Son of Man comes in His glory, and all the angels with Him, then He will sit on His glorious throne. All the nations will be gathered before Him; and He will separate them from one another, as the shepherd separates the sheep from the goats; and He will put the sheep on His right, and the goats on the left. Then the King will say to those on His right, 'Come, you who are blessed of My Father, inherit the kingdom prepared for you from the foundation of the world. For I was hungry, and you gave Me something to eat; I was thirsty, and you gave Me something to drink; I was a stranger, and you invited Me in; naked, and you clothed Me; I was sick, and you visited Me; I was in prison, and you came to Me.'

"Then the righteous will answer Him, 'Lord, when did we see You hungry, and feed You, or thirsty, and give You something to drink? And when did we see You a stranger, and invite You in, or naked, and clothe You? When did we see You sick, or in prison, and come to You?'

"The King will answer and say to them, 'Truly I say to you, to the extent that you did it to one of these brothers of Mine, even the least of them, you did it to Me'" (MT 25: 31–40).

This whole medieval notion of a King on a glorious throne who is apparently meant to be Jesus, and having all the nations bowing before Him and separating the sheep from the goats, and the whole concept of God loving some a lot but others not so much: all of that is so inconsistent with the rest of the Gospels, the afterlife evidence, and even the culture in which Jesus lived that it has to have been added later. Clinching this judgment is the fact that the whole ins-versus-outs storyline helps Church leaders to keep their flocks in line.

But the lesson within that shell of coal is true! We cannot now know how Jesus originally framed His story. What we do know is that once we dispense with the notions of the King as our judge and some people being loved by God while others are not, we are left with the fact that when we are kind to the least important person we can find, we are doing something wonderful for God. Showing love and kindness to anyone is a beautiful gift of love to God because each of us is part of God. The core of that story is an eternal truth.

LEARNING MORE PERFECT SELF-LOVE

Of course, the other end of the Lord's crucial command to **"Love your neighbor as yourself"** (MT 22:39) is self-love, which turns out to be no less important than loving others. My own experience has been that as I have freed myself from religious fears and learned to better love the genuine God of which my mind is a part, I have begun to hold myself in higher esteem. That is likely also to be your experience. As you better internalize the extraordinary extent to which God loves you in particular, you will find yourself standing a little straighter. You will breathe more deeply. It is so much easier to learn to love others when you are doing that from the certain knowledge that you are a powerful eternal being and the best-beloved child of an infinitely powerful God! Learn first to **"Love the Lord your God with all your heart, and with all your soul, and with all your mind"** (MT 22:37). Once your love of God is perfected to this extent, then your love of yourself and of every other person on the face of the earth becomes an easier and a natural progression.

MAKING LEARNING TO LOVE OUR PRIORITY

In order for us to love others in the way that God wants us to love others, it is essential that we internalize the fact that all of us are part of God. Once you have that fact so firmly in mind that you are looking at every human face and beginning to see divinity within it, here are a few exercises that might help:

1. ***Practice perfect love within your family.*** I have been married for forty-three years. Our marriage was rocky for awhile; there were times when I would have paid you to take him. But we've learned little ways to make one another happy. We've discovered that the first thirty years are the hardest. And as I look back now, I realize that even during the roughest times, we were teaching one another more and more about love. Your spouse, your children, and every other important person in your life all are people you chose before your birth to help you learn to love more perfectly. Unless there is real abuse involved, a lot of spiritual growth for both of you

can come from your seeing each relationship through.

2. ***Learn to forgive.*** We will talk about forgiving in the next chapter. There is a reason to learn to forgive which you will see is selfish, but it seems clear that one reason why Jesus stresses our need to learn to forgive is that forgiving those who have wronged us is a necessary precursor to loving them.

3. ***Learn to quell your anger.*** I have been an attorney for the owners of closely-held businesses for more than three decades. I noticed early in my career that many of these Type-A folks were yellers, but there also were business owners who had an unusual ability to keep control. I was friendly enough with one of them to ask him how he controlled his anger. He taught me a simple but powerful trick. He said that whenever he felt anger rising, he would very much slow and deepen his voice. I was at that time a harried working mother in a not-yet-wonderful marriage. In desperation, I began to use his trick. What amazed me was that within what I recall as only weeks, I stopped even really feeling anger!

Soon my negative-emotions meter was peaking at what you might call mild annoyance. By now, it is difficult for me to imagine the rage that I could feel before. Describing to you the difference this trick has made in my family and in my life would require a whole book by itself. Try it!

4. ***Spread your love for one person over groups of people.*** When my grandchildren were very young, I volunteered in each of their classrooms. There would be rows of little faces, and one of them would have a halo around it. I experimented with looking out over those classrooms and mechanically just taking that love, that specialness, that glow of my own grandchild and applying it to every child. I was volunteering only once a week, but I swear to you that within the month I would enter those classrooms and find that there was a halo around each little face! It was real love, too. Years later, while shopping, I came across a boy from my grandson's kindergarten class. He was so big now! I had to know how he was doing. He had no idea who I was, and his mother was looking

at me funny, but it was all I could do to keep from grabbing him into my arms.

5. ***Consider doing anonymous good deeds.*** Among the many things that you don't know about the eternal life to which you will return is that partying is very big there. When people return from having led lives of unusual spiritual growth, there are public celebrations and even parades. One communicator tells the story of a woman who must have died a hundred years ago, who had taken seriously Jesus's suggestion that when we give, we should try to do it secretly. **"But when you give to the poor, do not let your left hand know what your right hand is doing, so that your giving may be in secret; and your Father who sees what is done in secret will reward you"** (MT 6:3–4). This woman had made a practice of doing some small, secret kindness every day of her whole adult life. If she was discovered to be the giver on any day, that gift didn't count. She had to do something else. When she returned to what is our real home, she was astonished to find herself known and celebrated throughout all the afterlife levels.

There were parties and parades for her. My own experiments with anonymous giving suggest that as a habit, it makes you feel more kindly so it isn't a bad learning-to-love exercise. And then to boot there is the parade factor. If you want them to give you a parade in heaven, it turns out that doing many anonymous kindnesses on earth seems to be a way to make that happen.

Learning to love more perfectly is the purpose of every human life. It is the reason why you chose to include in your life the very annoyances that make you feel unloving. And believe it or not, perfection is the standard! Jesus tells us that repeatedly. It is the standard that will determine your level of spiritual development, and it is going to be the standard you apply when you look back during your life review. So you will be happier if you start striving now to perfect your ability to love everyone. As Jesus says, **"You have heard that it was said, 'You shall love your neighbor and hate your enemy.' But I say to you, love your enemies and pray for those who persecute you, so that you may be sons of your Father who is in heaven; for He causes His sun to rise on the evil and the good, and sends rain on the righteous and the unrighteous. For if you love those who love you, what reward do you** have? Do not even the tax collectors do the same? If you greet only your brothers, what more are you doing than others? Do not even the Gentiles do the same? Therefore you are to be perfect, as your heavenly Father is perfect" (MT 5:43–48).

Chapter Eight
Learning to Forgive is Important

Of course, learning to love gets top billing. It is our ability to love that will determine our degree of advancement in the afterlife levels. So learning to love is essential, but unless we also are experts at forgiveness, we are going to find that loving others in the nonjudgmental way that we are meant to love others is not going to be possible for us. So universal forgiveness must be mastered before we are able to perfectly love, and forgiving at that level is not easy.

There is another reason, too, why learning to better forgive is important for each of us. Learning to forgive the most horrendous offenses, easily and without a thought, is essential training for the certain moment when you are going to have to forgive yourself.

LIFE REVIEW AND JUDGMENT

A few afterlife-related facts are based in so much evidence, and the evidence is so consistent, that there can be no doubt those facts are true. And the evidence is overwhelming that neither God nor Jesus nor any other religious figure ever is our post-death judge. Instead, each of us will judge ourselves. So when you practice ever more perfect forgiveness, you are preparing yourself for the moment when you will need to find a way to forgive yourself.

Our judgment process is simple. Soon after we return to the afterlife levels, we gather with our spirit guides, who are the wonderful friends that helped us to make the most of this lifetime. Often there are elders as well. Together we review our life just lived. Where our life review happens, when it happens, who will be present, and other details are personal to each of us, and they seem to be designed to help us have the most constructive experience possible. Those who have described their own life reviews have talked about something like a holographic review of their entire lives. They felt as if they were living again every one of the emotions they had felt as their lives unfolded here, and they felt as well every emotion that they ever had engendered in anyone else.

Many of the dead tell us that feeling the way they had made others feel during the lifetime just completed was the worst experience that we can imagine. They had been prepared to see the big things they had done wrong, but what upset them was reliving all the many times when they had hurt other people's feelings, or caused sadness or disappointment, or even just passed up the chance to do for someone else some little kindness.

The atmosphere of our life review is always supportive. No matter what we may have done in our lives, no one condemns us for it. There is no need for anyone else to point out our mistakes, since we are back in our superconscious minds by then. We know what we had planned for the life just ended in the way of learning and spiritual growth. We can see all the ways in which we screwed that up.

Forgiveness is an essential part of every life review. We are asked to forgive everyone who ever harmed us in our lives, and by every account that I have seen, our forgiveness of others is immediate and complete. Forgive the guard at Auschwitz who murdered your family? No problem! From the perspective of our eternal lives, we realize that it all was a kind of play, everyone we love is fine, and indeed some of those we hated most in our lives have turned out to be our eternal friends who simply played a role in that lifetime in order to help us to better grow spiritually.

So apparently we forgive everyone immediately. That part of our life review is easy! The really difficult part comes next. We are told that now it is time to forgive ourselves.

Forgiving yourself for having fallen short of your own aspirations for spiritual growth in the lifetime just completed can be hard. There is counseling available to you in an atmosphere of love and acceptance. But if you can't manage self-forgiveness, you soon will face a terrible problem. Your spiritual vibratory rate will slow, so before long you won't be able to remain on a beautiful Summerland afterlife level. If you still can't manage to forgive yourself, you might eventually end up on the lowest afterlife level, what Jesus called the outer darkness level.

"I say to you that many will come from east and west, and recline at the table with Abraham, Isaac and Jacob in the kingdom of heaven; but the sons of the kingdom will be cast out into the outer darkness; in that place there will be weeping and gnashing of teeth" (MT 8:11–12).

This is such an arresting description of the cold and smelly lowest afterlife level that reading this passage was one of my biggest eureka moments on the amazing afternoon when I compared the Gospels with the afterlife evidence and discovered that two thousand years ago, Jesus had told us most of what the dead are telling us now.

The evidence is strong that everyone in the outer darkness was put there by himself or herself. I never have heard of an exception. Some people are so full of post-death remorse that they simply beeline down, while others try to avoid the punishment level but find it impossible to forgive themselves for something they have done in life.

JESUS CONFIRMS THAT WE JUDGE OURSELVES

When I compared the afterlife evidence with the Gospels and found Jesus talking about God's judgment, I worried at first that on this point He might have been mistaken. But then I considered this series of quotations. Remember that Jesus had to be careful to avoid speaking against the prevailing religion, in which Jehovah God was our afterlife judge. So on four different days, and probably with four different sets of Temple guards on hand, He made statements that He relied upon His followers to put together:

"For if you forgive others for their transgressions, your heavenly Father will also forgive you. But if you do not forgive others, then your Father will not forgive your transgressions" (MT 6:14–15).

Oh. So God judges us, but God will forgive us so long as we forgive others. Fair enough.

"For not even the Father judges anyone, but He has given all judgment to the Son, so that all will honor the Son even as they honor the Father" (JN 5:22–23).

Jesus is now our judge? Great! He'll likely be easier on us.

"If anyone hears My sayings and does not keep them, I do not judge him; for I did not come to judge the world, but to save the world" (JN 12:47).

Jesus isn't our judge either? So, now who will judge us?

"Do not judge so that you will not be judged. For in the way you judge, you will be judged; and by your standard of measure, it will be measured to you" (MT 7:1–2).

Jesus has had to wean his first-century followers from their old belief that God is their judge, and he has had to do it over days of time for fear of the ever-present Temple guards, but at last he is able to tell us flat-out what modern afterlife evidence demonstrates is true: each of us will be our own post-death judge. And unless we learn to be lenient with others, we are going to be too hard on ourselves.

ASK FOR FORGIVENESS—AND FORGIVE— BEFORE ANYONE DIES

If you believe that you have harmed someone during this lifetime, you would be well advised to apologize now and seek forgiveness. Otherwise, there is evidence that you may find it impossible to move on. I know of a number of people, including my own father, who seem to have avoided the outer darkness, but who nevertheless remained unable to fully resume their Summerlsnd lives until they could manage their post-death apologies. All the cases of which I am aware involved wrongs done to children. And in my father's situation, getting up the nerve to say the words took him twenty years.

My father died in 1991. When I was doing extensive research with spiritual mediums in the late nineties, many of them described him lurking nearby in his seventies-era plaid sport coat and fedora. Oddly, however, all of them told me that he refused to speak. Perhaps his pride wouldn't let him apologize when other family members were nearby. Then, twenty years almost to the day after his death, my father showed up in a session with a medium that I had given as a gift to my daughter. He said, **"Please ask your mother and her sister to forgive me for messing up their childhood."**

Now, my father was an alcoholic. Admittedly, there were some unpleasant moments, but overall I had a lovely childhood! If I had for a moment guessed that the poor man was going to blame himself for anything, I would have made certain before his death that he knew that I forgave him and I loved him.

Make your apologies now. Forgive everything now! Get yourself as right as you can right now, before death makes it harder for you to make your peace. As Jesus says, **"Therefore if you are presenting your offering at the altar, and there remember that your brother has something against you, leave your offering there before the altar and go; first be reconciled to your brother, and then come and present your offering"** (MT 5:23–24).

FORGIVING OUR ENEMIES

Forgiving the big and little bruises that come from human interactions is a necessary precursor to our learning to love perfectly. Holding grudges against family or friends gets in the way of our loving them, so even in happy family situations, the need to forgive keeps coming up. This is intimate forgiveness, the simple overlooking of negative interactions with the people we love. And it is basic stuff!

It's kindergarten. The kind of forgiveness that learning to love perfectly requires of us is quite a bit harder.

Jesus pays particular attention to our need to forgive not just friends and family members who annoy us, and not just the random acts of strangers, but also, and perhaps especially, deliberate wrongs that were done to us by people we might think of as outright enemies. He says, **"But I say to you, do not resist an evil person; but whoever slaps you on your right cheek, turn the other to him also. If anyone wants to sue you and take your shirt, let him have your coat also. Whoever forces you to go one mile, go with him two"** (MT 5:39–41).

"But love your enemies, and do good, and lend, expecting nothing in return; and your reward will be great, and you will be sons of the Most High; for He Himself is kind to ungrateful and evil men. Be merciful, just as your Father is merciful" (LK 6:35–36).

Learning to forgive the most evil acts committed against us with malice is a necessary precursor to our learning to love perfectly. Let's look at how we might best learn that lesson.

LEARNING RADICAL FORGIVENESS

Jesus talks a lot about the importance of learning to forgive automatically. His disciple, Peter, asked him, **"Lord, how**

often shall my brother sin against me and I forgive him? Up to seven times?" Jesus said to him, **"I do not say to you, up to seven times, but up to seventy times seven"** (MT 18:21–23).

No matter how many times someone does you wrong, you are meant to forgive without a thought. Every time. And actually, perhaps oddly, forgiving automatically turns out to be easier than the alternative. Until we learn to do what we will here call radical forgiveness, the forgiveness process requires us to notice each wrong, feel the pain of it, tamp down that pain, swallow hard, and manage to forgive the wrong anyway. It's a horse-and-buggy kind of forgiveness, a bespoke forgiveness that you tailor for each situation, and it takes a lot of distracting mental effort.

By contrast, once you learn to forgive automatically, you can get to the point where you hardly even notice whatever someone else did wrong. For all of us, this is our goal! Jesus and the dead who communicate with us all urge us to focus on learning to forgive every wrong ever done by anyone, no matter how life-changing it might be, as if it never happened at all.

Think about that!

We are meant to learn automatic, reflexive, universal, and complete forgiveness.

Here are some important facts to keep in mind about the process of radical forgiveness:

1. ***Forgiveness is not approval.*** If someone harms you or harms someone you love, or even if you learn about someone who has notoriously harmed a stranger, immediate and complete forgiveness is essential. You needn't (and you likely shouldn't) try to approve of whatever wrong was done.

2. ***You don't have to keep the offender in your life.*** In family situations, it may be important that you forgive and then work to rebuild the relationship, but otherwise it is fine if you forgive from the heart and release the offender with your love and blessing. And if a relationship is abusive or damaging, it's okay to forgive privately and separate yourself altogether.

3. ***Forgiveness is for you.*** Except within families, the wrongdoer likely doesn't care whether you forgive. Forgiveness is never for the other person, but rather forgiveness is your gift to yourself. And what a gift it is! As you learn to do it better,

you will find that practicing radical forgiveness makes you feel light and free. Even joyous.

4. ***Forgiveness becomes ever easier.*** When I first came to understand the importance of forgiving every wrong, I was an Olympics-level holder of grudges. To be alive was to keep score! Now at last, after years of trying, I have begun to master radical forgiveness. The difference is like setting down a hundred pounds of unnecessary garbage so you can dance your way through life.

5. ***There is no wrong that cannot be forgiven.*** When you treat forgiveness as an exercise that is essential to your spiritual health, you will find that, from the perspective of learning to forgive every wrong, there is not much difference between a stubbed toe and a murder. Human minds are eternal! When measured against forever, these unpleasant interactions with others on earth really amount to precisely nothing.

So, how do we begin to learn radical forgiveness? The easiest way to do it feels like a physical process. What I did in the beginning was to package each wrong in my mind. I would imagine that I was gathering every bit of it up and wrapping it all together. Then I would think, "I forgive and release!" and let it go. I would let it go physically: I envisioned myself pushing it away. Sometimes the darned thing would come right back, so I would have to go through the process again. In the beginning, I had to do this whenever I felt the least bit of resentment, but soon I was finding that my resentment was rising less and less often. By now, my forgiveness is so automatic that I seldom give it a thought.

Outrage turns out to be a lot like anger. If you court it and let yourself feel it, you are going to feel a lot more of it; but if you refuse to give it mind-space, you will find that soon it doesn't bother to get started. You still notice the wrong, and you recall how that sort of thing used to wreck your day, but now it doesn't bother you at all.

"Do not judge, and you will not be judged; and do not condemn, and you will not be condemned; pardon, and you will be pardoned. Give, and it will be given to you. They will pour into your lap a good measure— pressed down, shaken together, and running over. For by your standard of measure it will be measured to you in return" (LK 6:37–38).

Learning automatic and complete forgiveness is the foundation of your spiritual growth. It makes your life easier. And so much happier!

CHAPTER NINE
SPIRITUAL GROWTH IS THE PURPOSE OF HUMAN LIFE

The dead tell us that our life on earth is a school where we learn to better love and forgive as we work toward greater spiritual growth. Learning these lessons is why we live in families, why we are crowded enough to have to deal with others, why some of those that we deal with do us wrong, and why bad things happen to good people. Every occurrence in your life is either love or a call for love, so no matter what the question might be, love will always be the answer.

Or you might think of this process in more contemporary terms. Coming into a body is like spending a tough afternoon in a gym, where each obstacle in your life—each job setback, each death of a child, each evil mother-in-law or nasty neighbor—is like a weight-training machine that helps you strengthen a targeted set of spiritual muscles. For you to remain in the perfection of heaven would be like lolling around on a spiritual couch. It is only when you come to earth and experience the trials of earth-life that you are able to achieve rapid spiritual growth.

And, make no mistake. When you are in what we call the afterlife levels and in active contact with the parts of your mind that you can't directly access when in a body, you crave spiritual growth like every craving you ever have felt in your life at once. Like food and drink and sex, like a baby in your arms or financial success, you pine for what the dead tell us is the greatest possible thrill: you yearn for more intimate communion with God. So, as much as you are thinking now that you never will choose to go through this again, inevitably you will want another earth-lifetime. Everyone does. Until we reach a level of spiritual fitness that will let us serve others while remaining in the afterlife levels as we continue to work toward our spiritual perfection, we eagerly line up for more time on earth.

THE KINGDOM OF HEAVEN

One thing that seems to confuse people is that Jesus refers to our need to do certain things or we will not enter the Kingdom of Heaven. (The Kingdom of God might be an alternative term, but it seems to signal greater perfection so that is the interpretation that we will use here.) Does Jesus's telling us that our entry to the Kingdom of Heaven takes spiritual effort mean that not everybody goes to heaven?

Of course not. The afterlife evidence indicates that everyone who has lived a halfway reasonable life will wind up on at least the third afterlife level, which is the lowest of the beautiful Summerland levels. No worries! But Level Three is the floor. Jesus came to earth to tell us that we should be aiming for the ceiling, and to teach us the best way to hit that mark. A close examination of all His teachings suggests that what he means by the Kingdom of Heaven is something like Level Six, which is attainable only by those who are quite spiritually advanced. And if He is making a distinction between terms, then the Kingdom of God would be Level Seven, the Celestial Level, a beyond-joyous return to our Source.

Achieving even the Kingdom of Heaven requires that we learn to love and forgive at a level that approaches perfection. It requires that we love and forgive so perfectly that we never again look at a human face without seeing the divinity of which we all are a part; that we never again feel a nudge of annoyance if someone deliberately does us wrong. And we can get there. It just takes work!

"You have heard that the ancients were told, 'You shall not commit murder' and 'Whoever commits murder shall be liable to the court.' But I say to you that everyone who is angry with his brother shall be guilty before the court; and whoever says to his brother, 'You

good-for-nothing,' shall be guilty before the supreme court" (MT 5:21–22).

"But love your enemies, and do good, and lend, expecting nothing in return; and your reward will be great, and you will be sons of the Most High; for He Himself is kind to ungrateful and evil men. Be merciful, just as your Father is merciful" (LK 6:35–36).

"You have heard that it was said, 'You shall love your neighbor and hate your enemy.' But I say to you, love your enemies and pray for those who persecute you, so that you may be sons of your Father who is in heaven; for He causes His sun to rise on the evil and the good, and sends rain on the righteous and the unrighteous. For if you love those who love you, what reward do you have? Do not even the tax collectors do the same? If you greet only your brothers, what more are you doing than others? Do not even the Gentiles do the same? Therefore you are to be perfect, as your heavenly Father is perfect" (MT 5:43–48).

REINCARNATION

Jesus agrees with the dead in telling us that the standard for our spiritual growth is perfection. We are meant to become like God. **"You are to be perfect, as your heavenly Father is perfect"** (MT 5:48). Perfection is a difficult goal to achieve, and made more difficult by the fact that until we are fairly advanced beings, significant spiritual growth seems to happen only on this material plane. For nearly all of us, it requires many earth-lifetimes, each with its own set of basic lessons in ever more perfect love and forgiveness.

So reincarnation happens. And it is a good thing that we can keep coming back, since for us to build into a single lifetime sufficient lessons to achieve God's perfection would be not only painful, but downright impossible. Why didn't Jesus talk about reincarnation in the Gospels? He did talk about it, as you will see below. And there is evidence that He said more about it, but one of the early Church councils chose to remove from the Gospels what references it could find to reincarnation so people would believe they had just one lifetime and they would try their very best.

Pause and think about that. Just that single fact about those who put the Christian Bible together—the arrogance; the foolishness—tells you everything you need to know about how impossible it is for the entire Christian Bible to be the Inspired Word of God. When you read about these early councils' deliberations, the debates and the arbitrary setting in stone of notions that should have been discovered as facts, you find yourself sympathizing with Jesus as perhaps you never have before. He brought to His first followers a philosophy directly from God that would at last enable people in bodies to achieve very rapid spiritual growth. And then He had to watch from the afterlife levels as people who didn't take His teachings seriously enough to want to keep them intact argued about His virgin birth and whether or not He was actually God. Poor Jesus! And poor us.

So nearly all references to reincarnation in the Gospels have been edited out, and those that remain have been interpreted by Christians in light of traditions that have no support in the afterlife evidence and have nothing to do with Jesus.

For example, "Jesus said, **'Truly, truly, I say to you, unless one is born again he cannot see the kingdom of God.'**

"Nicodemus said to Him, **'How can a man be born when he is old? He cannot enter a second time into his mother's womb and be born, can he?'**

"Jesus answered, **'Truly, truly, I say to you, unless one is born of water and the Spirit he cannot enter into the kingdom of God. That which is born of the flesh is flesh, and that which is born of the Spirit is spirit. Do not be amazed that I said to you, "You must be born again." The wind blows where it wishes and you hear the sound of it, but do not know where it comes from and** where it is going; so is everyone who is born of the Spirit'" (JN 3:3–8).

This conversation refers to reincarnation. Jesus was telling Nicodemus that people need more than one earth-lifetime in order to advance spiritually to the point where they can enter the highest afterlife level, what Jesus refers to as the Kingdom of God. **"That which is born of the flesh is flesh, and that which is born of the Spirit is spirit"** refers to the fact that a body is only a fleshly vehicle for the precious part of Spirit that enters and briefly uses that body. Anyone who has witnessed a birth understands that being **"born of water and the Spirit"** would not be a bad description of it. And here is the most telling passage: **"The wind blows wherever it pleases. You hear its sound, but you cannot tell where it comes from or where it is going. So it is with everyone born of the Spirit."** This beautifully points to the fact that when our eternal minds are without material bodies between lives on earth, we are spirits that are free to move as we like and to contact those we love. They can hear us, but we are as invisible to them as the wind. If the Christian interpretations of this conversation were correct, then this important passage would be meaningless.

Christians, of course, have interpreted that exchange of Jesus with Nicodemus, the righteous Pharisee, to mean that baptism is required for entrance into heaven and that when we accept Jesus as our personal Savior, we are "born again." Neither of these Christian beliefs is supported by either the afterlife evidence or the rest of the Gospels, but it is Christianity and not Jesus that is in error. As we can see, a plain reading of this passage shows it to be a reference to reincarnation that was obscure enough that the early Church councils overlooked it.

HUMILITY IS ESSENTIAL FOR SPIRITUAL GROWTH

The dead tell us that our earth-status counts for nothing in the afterlife levels. Jesus agrees with them. **"Many who are first will be last, and the last, first"** (MK 10:31). **"The greatest among you shall be your servant. Whoever exalts himself shall be humbled; and whoever humbles himself shall be exalted"** (MT 23:11–12).

Jesus uses children as exemplars for the attitude that we should have if we hope to achieve real spiritual growth. **"Whoever receives this child in My name receives Me, and whoever receives Me receives Him who sent Me; for the one who is least among all of you, this is the one** who is great" (LK 9:48). **"Permit the children to come to Me; do not hinder them; for the kingdom of God belongs to such as these. Truly I say to you, whoever does not receive the kingdom of God like a child will not enter it at all"** (MK 10:14–15).

We know little about those few people who have attained the Celestial Level of spiritual development, but we do know that they have managed to burn out their human egos altogether. Until we achieve the degree of childlike humility that is possible only when we are devoid of the petty demands of ego, and even if our managing that takes us beyond an eternity of time, we will not be able to enter Level Seven. We will miss out on the boundless joy of eventual reunion with our Source.

SPIRITUAL GROWTH IS BASED IN LOVE

Spiritual growth is more complex than love alone, but loving God, ourselves, and all of humanity is its indispensable base. Until we have mastered universal love, no amount of meditation or self-mortification or religious practice or charitable giving or even every effort put together is going to avail us much in our efforts to grow spiritually. Perfect universal love is not a rule to be mechanically followed. Rather, it is a way of thinking that must altogether fill our minds, so we never again have any thought nor do even the smallest thing that is not the fruit of a heart full of love.

"A new commandment I give to you, that you love one another, even as I have loved you, that you also love one another" (JN 13:34).

"'You shall love the Lord your God with all your heart, and with all your soul, and with all your mind.' This is the great and foremost commandment. The second is like it, 'You shall love your neighbor as yourself.' On these two commandments depend the whole Law and the Prophets" (MT 22:37–40).

Jesus is telling us that if we hope to make spiritual progress, we must live by love, and only by love, in everything we do and no matter what anyone who is not governed by love might do to us. It's a difficult standard! But our job as followers of Jesus is to learn perfect universal love, and to demonstrate His philosophy of perfect love as the greatest gift that we can give to a stumbling and despairing world.

UNLESS WE CONTINUE TO MAKE SPIRITUAL PROGRESS, WE WILL FALL BACKWARD

Jesus says some things in the Gospels that seem incomprehensible and even cruel until we realize that what He is referring to is not earthly riches, but spiritual ones.

"For to everyone who has, more shall be given, and he will have an abundance; but from the one who does not have, even what he does have shall be taken away. Throw out the worthless slave into the outer darkness; in that place there will be weeping and gnashing of teeth" (MT 25:29–30).

"For nothing is hidden that will not become evident, nor anything secret that will not be known and come to light. So take care how you listen; for whoever has, to him more shall be given; and whoever does not have, even what he thinks he has shall be taken away from him" (LK 8:17–18).

Jesus isn't talking here about material wealth. He is referring to spiritual growth, which from His perspective is the one thing worth having. And these are not God's arbitrary rules. Rather, they are scientific precepts in a reality governed by the physics of consciousness. As inevitable as the tug of gravity and as inexorable as the temperature at which water freezes is the fact that if we stop making spiritual progress, we risk losing whatever spiritual growth we might already have attained.

"Do not store up for yourselves treasures on earth, where moth and rust destroy, and where thieves break in and steal. But store up for yourselves treasures in heaven, where neither moth nor rust destroys, and where thieves do not break in or steal; for where your treasure is, there your heart will be also" (MT 6:19–21).

Jesus warns us often against being distracted and seduced by earthly baubles. This lifetime on earth will be over in no time! And when you are again entering the lowest level of the Summerland, glad to be returning to your true home, then all the wealth and power, fame and glory, and every conceivable material pleasure that you battled during your lifetime to possess will be revealed to have been dross. You will wish with all that is in you that you had spurned what has no spiritual value and invested your precious time on earth in wealth that you could take with you! Spiritual wealth is the only wealth there is. **"Again, the kingdom of heaven is like a merchant seeking fine pearls, and upon finding one pearl of great value, he went and sold all that he had and bought it"** (MT 13:45–46).

And what is our eventual goal?

"Blessed are the poor in spirit, for theirs is the kingdom of heaven . . . Blessed are the pure in heart, for they shall see God" (MT 5:3, 8).

Some have asked what the words "poor in spirit" mean in this context. It's clear from all the teachings of Jesus that "poor in spirit" means humble, gentle, loving, forgiving, and clear of ego-based complications. Once we have spiritually progressed that far, we can be comfortable at vibratory levels as high as Level Six of the afterlife. We are ready to begin to make progress toward what we are told is the greatest pleasure there is: sufficient purity of heart that we are capable of direct communion with God.

WE MUST WALK THE WALK, NOT JUST TALK THE TALK

Jesus says, **"But what do you think? A man had two sons, and he came to the first and said, 'Son, go work today in the vineyard.' And he answered, 'I will not'; but afterward he regretted it and went. The man came to the second and said the same thing; and he answered, 'I will, sir'; but he did not go. Which of the two did the will of his father? . . . Truly I say to you that the tax collectors and prostitutes will get into the kingdom of God before you"** (MT 21:28–31).

It is not enough to sit in church on Sundays. It is not enough to pray in the name of Jesus. And certainly it is not enough to claim that the death of Jesus has "saved" us. When it comes to our spiritual growth, good intentions amount to precisely nothing. Jesus was massively frustrated to see his followers revering Him while ignoring His teachings. Imagine what He would say to us today!

"Why do you call me 'Lord, Lord,' and do not do what I say?" (LK 6:46). **"Not everyone who says to me, 'Lord, Lord,' will enter the kingdom of heaven, but he who does the will of my Father who is in heaven will enter"** (MT 7:21). Patiently he keeps on making it clear that, **"If you continue in My word, then you are truly disciples of Mine; and you will know the truth, and the truth will make you free"** (JN 8:31–32).

WE ARE MEANT TO BE GOOD STEWARDS OF OUR OWN SPIRITUAL GROWTH

It isn't up to God to magically bestow upon us the gift of spiritual growth. Whether we make spiritual progress or not is entirely in our own hands. And it's not easy! There are no shortcuts. Jesus tells parables to help his followers grasp this essential point. He is talking here of our attainment of the Kingdom of Heaven, by which He means spiritual growth sufficient to let us reach the upper afterlife levels and live in joyous proximity to our Source.

"For it is just like a man about to go on a journey, who called his own slaves and entrusted his possessions to them. To one he gave five talents, to another, two, and to another, one, each according to his own ability; and he went on his journey. Immediately the one who had received the five talents went and traded with them, and gained five more talents. In the same manner the one who had received the two talents gained two more. But he who received the one talent went away, and dug a hole in the ground and hid his master's money.

"Now after a long time the master of those slaves came and settled accounts with them. The one who had received the five talents came up and brought five more talents, saying, 'Master, you entrusted five talents to me. See, I have gained five more talents.' His master said to him, 'Well done, good and faithful servant. You were faithful with a few things, I will put you in charge of many things; enter into the joy of your master.'

"Also the one who had received the two talents came up and said, 'Master, you entrusted two talents to me. See, I have gained two more talents.' His master said to him, 'Well done, good and faithful servant. You were faithful with a few things, I will put you in charge of many things; enter into the joy of your master.'

"And the one also who had received the one talent came up and said, 'Master, I knew you to be a hard man, reaping where you did not sow and gathering where you scattered no seed. And I was afraid, and went away and hid your talent in the ground. See, you have what is yours.'

"But his master answered and said to him, 'You wicked, lazy slave, you knew that I reap where I did not sow and gather where I scattered no seed. Then you ought to have put my money in the bank, and on my arrival I would have received my money back with interest. Therefore take away the talent from him, and give it to the one who has the ten talents.'

"For to everyone who has, more shall be given, and he will have an abundance; but from the one who does not have, even what he does have shall be taken away. Throw out the worthless slave into the outer darkness; in that place there will be weeping and gnashing of teeth" (MT 25:14–30).

This is an important parable! Our spiritual nature is an extraordinary gift from God, but it is only the beginning of what is possible for us. Our task is to nurture our spiritual nature and build upon it throughout our lives, so when we graduate back to where we live eternally, we will have used whatever degree of spiritual development we might have carried into this lifetime to gain even much more spiritual growth. Then we will rejoice to hear those beautiful words: **"Well done, good and faithful servant!"**

The Lord persistently tells us that our spiritual growth is our own responsibility. No one else, and no religious shortcut, has the power to do it for us. But each of us has the personal power to advance spiritually, lifetime by lifetime. And the whole heavenly host is rooting for us. Jesus says, **"What man among you, if he has a hundred sheep and has lost one of them, does not leave the ninety-nine in the open pasture and go after the one which is lost until he finds it? When he has found it, he lays it on his shoulders, rejoicing. And when he comes home, he calls together his friends and his neighbors, saying to them, 'Rejoice with me, for I have found my sheep which was lost!' I tell you that in the same way, there will be more joy in heaven over one sinner who repents than over ninety-nine righteous persons who need no repentance"** (LK 15:4–7).

MY OWN EXPERIMENT

I am not especially good. For most of my life I have been self-absorbed and heedless of the needs of others, to the point where my decision in 2009 to give the rest of my life to God may have been rooted in my realization that it was time for me to clean up my act. As I wonder now about the astonishing events that I share with you in Appendix V, and why on earth I was chosen for this task and not someone who is a lot more perfect, it occurs to me that the fact that I am so flawed but I am attempting now to grow spiritually might make it easier for me to help you along the same path.

It was only about three years ago that I began to try to take the teachings of the Lord as seriously as He means them to be taken. And it was hard at first! You've got to keep squelching negative feelings by force and reminding yourself that, yep, even this or that venal nuisance of a human being also is a part of God. Fortunately, though, I have found that the process of following the Lord is self-reinforcing. Even now, I don't feel negative emotions as frequently or as deeply as I did before, and I find that with only minimal thought I can dispel them. They no longer take root. I have begun to feel lighter all the time, more deeply peaceful, more happily loving toward everyone on the face of the earth.

Already I feel amazingly different. Already. And I was old when I began this exercise! I can only imagine how much spiritually richer my whole life could have been if the religion to which I was so devoted had taught me from childhood how to follow my Teacher. If we do nothing more, it is essential that from this day forward we share the teachings of Jesus with the children!

When You Live the Lord's Teachings, Amazing Things Can Happen

I have never been remotely psychic. For my whole adult life I have studied the afterlife and the greater reality to which we graduate at death from the viewpoint of the experiences of others, unable even to imagine what it would be like to communicate directly with Spirit. Then one day my long-ignored spirit guide asked spiritual medium Susanne Wilson to arrange a meeting with me. In an amazing conversation through Susanne, Thomas told me some of his history. He talked about the effort now underway to raise the consciousness of the planet, and in furtherance of that goal he asked me to help him write a book about Jesus. Since he last had been in body in the 1800s, he said that he would give me the ideas. My job would be to tailor his message to better suit the modern world.

To be utterly non-psychic all your life and approaching seventy years of age when you are told that you are about to channel a book is a genuine giggle. Our primary spirit guides are so close to us that they nearly are aspects of ourselves, so when I started to help Thomas with his book it felt as if it was all my doing. The ideas just were forming easily. I felt of a sudden hugely smarter.

But my adventure into channeling my primary guide turned out to be just Spirit's test-drive. We were barely well started when one afternoon Susanne sent me an email saying that Thomas had seized her in a parking lot and given her a message for me. He had said, **"Please forgive the speed at which we are dictating, as your soul-ular self is working directly for the Master now, without benefit of the filters which would slow the transmission. And I hasten to add, you must please of course speak clearly should your physical suffer exhaustion."**

At two o'clock the following morning I woke up with a pressing need to write, and I sat down at my computer and began to channel Master Jesus. Working with Jesus was easier than you would imagine. His energy is that of the Source, but He toned it down a lot for me! He felt in my mind as if I had become of a sudden deeply calm and wise. He was such an expert at what we were doing that He was using my body as a word-processor, supplying not just the ideas but also many of the words and phrases. And He never stopped! I wrote all that night and all the next day before I begged Him to please let me sleep. Jesus worked so fast that I was scarcely aware of what I was writing, and I had no time to go back and read; sometimes He would pull me back, though, and keep making me look at something I had written until I realized what it was that He wanted me to change. Then He let me return to where we had left off, and He returned to downloading. Together we wrote a forty-thousand-word book in only two weeks of work.

The thing about extraordinary experiences is that while they are happening you are too immersed in them to distance yourself enough to marvel at what is going on. I did know it was Jesus. You know that, while it's happening. I was too much in awe to say much to Him beyond that first request that He allow for sleeping, but as He became more efficient at using me and the connection got stronger, sometimes I could hear Him talking to Himself. That part was amazing! It felt intimate, listening to the Lord's spoken thoughts. It made me sympathize deeply with Him, which is a word I never would have thought that you could find a reason to use for the Son of God. But He was asking to be listened to, asking to be understood, and that is such a deeply human need that hearing Him talk about it could make my eyes sting.

It was only when I woke up one morning bereft of Jesus that I knew that this book was finished. Within half a day my Thomas was back, and for two further months he had me tweaking and polishing what he and I both think of now as my beloved spirit guide's long-delayed book. Thomas and I did add a few things, especially in this chapter and the next, but we made no changes in the Lord's message. Most of what you hold in your hands is His work.

When you win the Lottery or you get into Harvard, you feel humbled. You might say, "Why me? When Jesus gives you a book to share with the world, that is something so far beyond humbling that I really never thought to ask, "Why me?" It was only when I sent Susanne Wilson the finished book because she is mentioned in it that her response made me realize the answer to the question I never had thought to ask. She sent me an email that said in part, **"I was amazed when Thomas jumped into my body to tell you, Roberta, that you are 'now working directly for the Master.' Even though I received the message loud and clear myself, it took my breath away. Why Roberta? Why now?**

"After much praying, I woke up the next morning with the answer. It's quite clear. The Creator wants to speak directly to anyone and everyone who's being obedient to His Law of Love. Jesus taught compassion in our thoughts, words, and actions. You are attuned to Him, Roberta. He wants all of us attuned. Your book

will help fan the flame of His love that dwells within each of us. We are all one."

Her message made me realize that the primary reason I was chosen likely is a simple one. Jesus used me because for the previous few years I had been trying to attune my life to His teachings. There is no way to know what is going to happen in your own life once you make living the Gospels the center of it, but I can attest that whatever happens will be wonderful! Those moments of hearing Jesus in my mind as He expressed His human need to be heard I will hold forever in my deepest heart.

OUR RELIGIONS SLIGHT OUR SPIRITUAL NEEDS

As they are practiced now, none of the great religions fosters our spiritual growth. Religions instill in us fear-based rules and irrelevant traditions. They create a template in our minds of acceptable behavior without giving us touchstones of truth against which to measure our thoughts and actions. They are mere form, meant just to mimic the appearance of spiritual growth. And they tend to make us judgmental and self-righteous, two human characteristics on heavy display among today's most ardent Christians that are the antithesis of spiritual growth.

"When you pray, go into your room, close the door and pray to your Father who is in secret, and your Father who sees what is done in secret will reward you" (MT 6:6). **"For nothing is hidden, except to be revealed; nor has anything been secret, but that it would come to light. If anyone has ears to hear, let him hear"** (MK 4:22–23). Each of us has by our very nature the most intimate possible relationship with God. God knows us to our deepest core. And God loves us, just as we are, much more than we can possibly imagine.

JESUS'S APPARENT MISSION

As I will tell you in Appendix V, I have it on good authority that Jesus actually is unique, so elevated that two thousand years ago God could walk the earth and look through His eyes to try to puzzle out how giving human beings free will could have gone so wrong. Beyond fact-finding, it was God's intention as Jesus to help us learn how to live our lives so we could at last begin to make optimal spiritual progress in each lifetime. As Jesus says, **"The words I say to you I do not speak on my own authority. Rather, it is the Father, living in me, who is doing his work"** (JN 14:10).

So the Gospel teachings of Jesus are a prescription directly from God for how we can make rapid spiritual progress. **"The word which you hear is not Mine, but the Father's who sent Me"** (JN 14:24). Jesus insists to us now that far from trying to establish just another religion, His mission was to abolish our need for religions by teaching us how to relate to God individually.

The Gospel words of Jesus suggest that He had five educational objectives:

First, He came to reveal to us the true nature of God.

Second, He came to show us how to relate to God individually.

Third, He came to teach us how to make the most spiritual progress while on Earth.

Fourth, He came to help us understand that our lives really are eternal.

And finally, He came to give us a taste of what the afterlife is like.

If these were His objectives, then His death and resurrection can be seen as a loving and joyous **"Ta-da!"** In rising spectacularly from the dead after a ghastly public execution, Jesus was demonstrating for simple people the fact that human lives are eternal. What looks like death isn't death at all.

CHAPTER TEN
BUILDING FOR JESUS THE MOVEMENT THAT HE INTENDED

I understand how hard it is to believe that the Christianity we have been practicing for two thousand years is not what Jesus had in mind. Perhaps you find it harder still to comprehend that Jesus didn't come to start a religion in the first place, but instead His teachings were meant to be a universal philosophy to assist all of humankind in achieving more rapid spiritual growth.

As difficult as all of this is to believe, the evidence that it is true is still where it has been for two thousand years, plain to see in the Lord's Gospel words themselves. When we read the four Gospels alone, taking care only to remove Christianity's later additions and distortions, we at last have the joy of coming to know our eternal Way-Shower and Best Friend.

God is real. All our minds are part of God, and Jesus told us two thousand years ago that we don't need religions coming between us and God. That unfortunately His nascent movement became just another fear-based religion and was stuck in time for two thousand years has only delayed the glorious moment when the words of Jesus can at last be heard.

REALLY LISTENING TO JESUS

Jesus is calling us now to listen to Him. He is asking us to free Him from the constraints of a religion that isn't based in His teachings and really give Him His chance to be heard. Jesus seems to be content that we stick to just the four canonical Gospels, the ones that were selected by those assembling the Bible, even though there is additional rich learning to be had in some of the Gospels that were rejected by the early Church. He is willing to stake His case to us on Matthew, Mark, Luke, and John. So He isn't asking for anything fancy. He just wants us to read His Gospels without the rest of the Bible in the way.

My first attempt at reading the Gospels by themselves was the greatest experience of my life. I met in those four books a gloriously living and beautiful Man, a Teacher who spoke to my heart as no one ever really had done before. I had thought for my whole life before that day that I was a follower of Jesus, but it was only when He called me out of the religion that bears His name and took me by the hand and showed me what more was possible for my life that I began to understand what it is to love Jesus.

Now Jesus is saying to each of us, **"Come to Me, all who are weary and heavy-laden, and I will give you rest. Take My yoke upon you and learn from Me, for I am gentle and humble in heart, and you will find rest for your souls. For My yoke is easy and My burden is light"** (MT 11:28–30).

I have found His promise to be not only true, but gloriously far beyond the greatest promise that ever before has been made by anyone, and with the grandest of all rewards. Unless you consider your life to be perfect and your spiritual development to be complete, I urge you for your own sake and for the sake of an exhausted and despairing world to give Jesus the chance to speak to you! Please:

- *Buy a red-letter version of a modern English translation of the Bible and read those red letters repeatedly.* I don't know about translations in other languages, but so long as you are careful to pick the bits of coal from among Thomas Jefferson's diamonds (see Appendix I), the Gospels in modern English are proven now by the afterlife evidence to be wonderfully, eternally true. Read the words of Jesus, and just for now read nothing in the Bible but the words of Jesus.

Give the Lord His chance to speak to you. Really listen to His words. And marvel.

- *Familiarize yourself with the afterlife evidence.* If you have been a Christian all your life, you may not realize how much your very being is steeped in fear by your religion. Once you fully grasp what we have learned from studying nearly two hundred years of abundant and consistent afterlife evidence, you will be able to replace those superstitious terrors with a glorious certainty of who and what you are and what the genuine God is. And then you will no longer fear anything.

THE ENTIRE WORLD NEEDS THE TEACHINGS OF JESUS

There has been no religion in human history that has much advanced our spiritual growth. And there seem to be three reasons for what we might see as this failure of all religions to effectively serve us spiritually:

1. *No religion focuses primarily on our need for spiritual growth.* Until we began to communicate actively with the dead in the latter part of the nineteenth century, very few of us had any concept of the meaning and purpose of

human life. Of course, Jesus flat-out told us everything we need to know two thousand years ago, and various other sages also have taught us things that we now can see were sound, but the human impulse has been to encase received wisdom in culture-based religions and to freeze them in the amber of time. If core teachings have been remembered at all, it has tended to be with mere lip-service.

2. *Religions are easy. Spiritual growth is harder.* All the great religions treat us like spiritual children. They give us rules to follow which mimic the behavior of people who are spiritually advanced, but they don't tell us how we can make spiritual progress on our own. They don't even tell us that spiritual growth is important! Rather, they complacently teach us that following their rules is going to be enough. The Christian doctrine of sacrificial redemption is a wonderful example of this tendency of religions to offer ineffectual spiritual shortcuts. Most Christian denominations promise their followers that whatever awful things they might have done, and no matter how much they hate their

fellow man, if they just claim Jesus as their personal savior they'll cut right to the head of heaven's line. This should long since have been seen as nonsense, but many Christians believe it to this day.

3. ***Religions are based in fear.*** Religions instill in us a great fear, whether of their version of God or simply of the unknown, and with that fear they package an easy way for us to comfort ourselves that we can use only if we remain in that religion. Christianity offers a prime example, but all religions work the same way. In Christianity, we learn that we carry from birth an original sin that will make God condemn us to hell, but if we practice the right kind of Christianity, we can be sure to escape God's wrath. That same combination of terror and beliefs-based salvation is at the core of all religions. And—I cannot say this often enough—if we fear God, we cannot love God as we must love God in order to make spiritual progress. For so long as we adhere to a fear-based religion, we are going to find it hard to leave the lowest rungs of our spiritual ladder.

Since achieving spiritual growth is the whole reason why we are born into bodies, there is no religion that is serving us well. So our need for the universal philosophy that is summarized in the teachings of Jesus is tremendous! This is especially true now that the dead are telling us that a Christian sect is about to present civilization with an existential danger. We are told that unless we give Jesus the chance to restate His case to the modern world, people who actually call themselves Christians will in about two hundred years be starting a cataclysmic war. But if sufficient people will assist Jesus in bringing His teachings to the modern world, then instead of the End Times in two hundred years, we can establish the Kingdom of God on earth. We can at last bring to pass the very outcome for which we have been praying ever since Jesus taught us to say, **"Your kingdom come. Your will be done, on earth as it is in heaven"** (MT 6:10).

And according to Jesus, it wouldn't take many people devoutly following Him now to avert the disaster of Biblical Armageddon and begin to bring about God's earthly Kingdom. We needn't even be showy about it. Our task is just to demonstrate God's perfect love in our own lives as we patiently share the truth of the Gospels. As Jesus says, **"The kingdom of heaven is like leaven, which a** woman took and hid in three pecks of flour until it was all leavened" (MT 13:33). It is our task now to become the Lord's leaven and spread His teachings to all the world.

Jesus is saying again to each of us, **"You are the salt of the earth; but if the salt has become tasteless, how can it be made salty again? It is no longer good for anything, except to be thrown out and trampled under foot by men.**

"You are the light of the world. A city set on a hill cannot be hidden; nor does anyone light a lamp and put it under a basket, but on the lampstand, and it gives light to all who are in the house. Let your light shine before men in such a way that they may see your good works, and glorify your Father who is in heaven" (MT 5:13–16).

These words of Jesus are familiar to Christians. Two thousand years later, they have not changed. What is new is that now we realize that Jesus really means what He says! And because we have recent afterlife evidence as independent confirmation, we can better understand what He is saying.

"You are the salt of the earth." You came into this lifetime with the divine gift of a spiritual nature that has been nurtured and grown through many earth-lifetimes and enables you now to further grow spiritually as you enrich the lives of others. But if you fail to care for and build your spiritual nature, you risk losing what growth and value you already have attained. **"You are the light of the world"** refers to spiritual light. **"Let your light shine before men in such a way that they may see your good works, and glorify your Father who is in heaven."** Jesus invites each of us to demonstrate His teachings in our own lives as we work together to enlighten the world. Every follower of Jesus is being called now to work hard at growing spiritually, and to share via teaching and loving demonstration the kind of spiritual perfection that will make possible the advent of the Kingdom of God on earth.

"How shall we picture the kingdom of God, or by what parable shall we present it? It is like a mustard seed, which, when sown upon the soil, though it is smaller than all the seeds that are upon the soil, yet when it is sown, it grows up and becomes larger than all the garden plants and forms large branches; so that the birds of the air can nest under its shade" (MK 4:30–32). That mustard seed of the Kingdom of God on earth is what Jesus tried to sow two thousand years ago. As He invites us to freshly share His teachings with everyone in the modern world, He is entrusting His new seed to you and me.

HOW MIGHT WE BEGIN TO SHARE THE LORD'S TRUTH?

If you really listen to Jesus, you may soon feel called to do His bidding as His first disciples were called to abandon their fishermen's nets when He said to them, **"Follow Me, and I will make you fishers of men"** (MT 4:19). He is making that call to many of us today. He is saying, **"Go therefore and make disciples of all the nations . . . teaching them to observe all that I commanded you"** (MT 28:19–20). Fortunately, since what Jesus shares in the Gospels is a philosophy and not a religion, there is no one on earth who should feel constrained by religious beliefs from listening to Him. And even the very religious need to hear what the Lord has to say!

Jesus does not even require that we enforce a uniform interpretation of His teachings. Some will accept His words with joy, and they may even begin to outdo His followers in thinking through how best to build ever more spiritually productive lives. Jesus tells us this is fine. It's wonderful! John, the disciple who was the Lord's close friend, once complained to him that, **"Master, we saw someone casting out demons in Your name; and we tried to prevent him because he does not follow along with us."**

But Jesus said to him, **"Do not hinder him; for he who is not against you is for you"** (LK 9:49–50).

Still, we must accept the fact that not everyone will be receptive to the truth that Jesus is asking us to teach. He says, **"Behold, the sower went out to sow; and as he sowed, some seeds fell beside the road, and the birds came and ate them up. Others fell on the rocky places, where they did not have much soil; and immediately they sprang up, because they had no depth of soil. But when the sun had risen, they were scorched; and because they had no root, they withered away. Others fell among the thorns, and the thorns came up and choked them out. And others fell on the good soil and yielded a crop, some a hundredfold, some sixty, and some thirty"** (MT 13:3–8).

The seed that Jesus sowed two thousand years ago fell into the thorns of the then-prevailing religion. It was consumed by ancient Judaism and transformed into a Jewish sect, its dogmas and traditions all established to be outgrowths of that millennia-old religion. Although Christians honor the name of Jesus, His teachings are not seen by them to have any better claim to being the Inspired Word of God than is Jehovah's Old Testament insistence that we kill anyone who violates the Sabbath (Exodus 35:2).

But the seed that Jesus is sowing now is going to fall upon good soil. With His guidance, we can see to that.

And unlike the fear- and guilt-based Christianity that we have for so long struggled to share, the Lord's simple teaching that we can develop a personal relationship with God and can learn to perfectly love and forgive and achieve ever greater spiritual growth is the most joyous philosophy that can be imagined! You and I, hand in hand with the Lord, have the power to transform the world.

You may be wondering what we ought to call this philosophy of Jesus that is not a religion. It might not even need a name, but Jesus and His disciples called it the Way (see, e.g., Acts 9:1). As He says, **"My teachings are the Way, and the truth, and the life. No one comes to the Father except through My teachings"** (JN 14:6). The Gospel teachings of Jesus are the Way for every human being on the face of the earth to make the most spiritual progress in this lifetime.

WE MUST BE GRATEFUL TO THE FIRST CHRISTIANS

As we begin to use the Gospels to transform our lives and to save the world, let's acknowledge our debt to the earliest Christians. When Saint Paul shaped a new religion that was suitable for his first-century followers, he built it around the Gospel teachings of Jesus, and thereby he preserved them. Jesus is making it clear to us now that Christianity is not what He intended. Christianity is not of Jesus, but if it were not for the work of those earliest Christians we wouldn't have the teachings of Jesus today. Thank you, Paul! And thank you, beautiful Christian martyrs. At last, all of humankind can open your gift.

Two thousand years ago, Jesus charged his followers to spread his teachings to all nations. He is making His charge to us again today. He says, **"All authority has been given to Me in heaven and on earth. Go therefore and make disciples of all the nations . . . teaching them to observe all that I commanded you; and lo, I am with you always, even to the end of the age"** (MT 28:19–20).

Appendices

Appendix I
Plucking Bits of Coal from among the Diamonds

The words of Jesus in the Bible are "as easily distinguishable as diamonds in a dunghill."
—Thomas Jefferson

When we were treating the whole Christian Bible as the Inspired Word of God, we were stuck with accepting whatever those Bible words might say. Now we understand, however, that none of the Bible is magically the Inspired Word of God. Now we are able to verify by using nearly two centuries' worth of afterlife evidence that only the Gospels can be independently corroborated. We are even able to further refine what within the Gospels themselves Jesus likely did and did not say.

Fortunately, most of what Jesus is quoted as saying in the Gospels can be seen to be consistent with the afterlife evidence and with other things He is reported to have said. But still, there are bits of coal that a careful reader can distinguish and pluck from among what Thomas Jefferson referred to as the diamond words of Jesus. And it is important that we make an effort to discover and remove that coal, since in some cases it very much distorts the actual message of Jesus.

Truth is truth! And only the truth is what Jesus wants to put into our hands. In general, if something Jesus is quoted as saying in the Gospels is (a) inconsistent with the afterlife evidence; (b) inconsistent with other things that Jesus is quoted as saying in the Gospels; and perhaps even (c) just what those who were establishing Christianity would have wanted Jesus to say, then chances are good that we have spotted some coal.

HERE ARE A FEW EXAMPLES

As you read and reread the Gospel red letters, you will become ever better at distinguishing those passages that simply do not fit with the rest. What has felt beautiful about this process for me is that in trying to sort wheat from chaff in the Gospels, I have had to examine the red letters closely. In doing that, I have come to know Jesus as I never had before. His love, His wisdom, and the astonishing perfection of His teachings shine ever brighter. His words in the Gospels are diamonds, indeed!

I should especially note that as we have studied the afterlife evidence, we have come to know the genuine God as perfect, universal love devoid of human failings. So anything that makes God seem to be less than perfect cannot have come from Jesus. In addition, of course, any reference in the Gospels to "thrones," the "elect," the "end times," or "sin" as the breaking of arbitrary rules is derived from Christian theology and therefore must be a later edit.

- It is important to be alert for terms that are anachronistic, erroneous, or doctrinal. In the passage quoted below, we notice the anachronistic reference to a "church," the erroneous reference to a gated Hades, the impossible reference to handing "the keys of the Kingdom of Heaven" to a human being, the notion of "binding" on earth being in any way applicable to heaven, and of course the fact that this passage is exactly what the church-builders would have wanted Jesus to say. Here is the most blatant later addition of them all:

"I also say to you that you are Peter, and upon this rock I will build My church; and the gates of Hades will not overpower it. I will give you the keys of the kingdom of heaven; and whatever you bind on earth shall have been bound in heaven, and whatever you loose on earth shall have been loosed in heaven" (MT 16:18–19).

This next example is inconsistent with both the afterlife evidence and the meaning and tone of most other Gospel passages. It gives clergymen a handy threat to keep their flocks in line. It inserts the idea of a cross long before Jesus died on one. It warns us that we might lose our soul, when in fact that is impossible. And the last sentence is an anachronistic and erroneous reference to events imagined in the Book of Revelation. This passage is a particularly unpleasant lump of coal that we can gladly toss:

"Then Jesus said to His disciples, **'If anyone wishes to come after Me, he must deny himself, and take up his cross and follow Me. For whoever wishes to save his life will lose it; but whoever loses his life for My sake will find it. For what will it profit a man if he gains the whole world and forfeits his soul? Or what will a man give in exchange for his soul? For the Son of Man is going to come in the glory of His Father with His angels, and will then repay every man according to his deeds'"** (MT 16:24–27).

- Some bits of coal are given away by their references to theological concepts that would have been unknown to Jesus. For example, the whole notion of a Trinity was proposed only after Jesus was crucified. Every Trinitarian reference in the Gospels therefore is a frank anachronism. So we must remove what would otherwise be an important sentence from the Great Commission:

"And Jesus came up and spoke to them, saying, **'All authority has been given to Me in heaven and on earth.**

Go therefore and make disciples of all the nations, *(baptizing them in the name of the Father and the Son and the Holy Spirit,)* **teaching them to observe all that I commanded you; and lo, I am with you always, even to the end of the age'"** (MT 28:18–20).

- *Some obvious coal is cultural.* When a passage has medieval details and a medieval feel to it, and especially if it doesn't fit particularly well with either the rest of the Gospels or the afterlife evidence, then we have found a later edit. The core of this story, that what we do for the least person we are doing for Jesus, is beautiful, and it is true. But all this talk of a King and a throne and nations gathering must be later cultural edits. The notion that Jesus will return "in His glory" smacks of a fictitious End Times. And of course, the afterlife evidence and the Gospel words of Jesus insist that each of us is perfectly loved and neither God nor Jesus ever will judge us, so all that nonsense about sheep and goats gets pitched into the dustbin as well:

"But when the Son of Man comes in His glory, and all the angels with Him, then He will sit on His glorious throne. All the nations will be gathered before Him; and He will separate them from one another, as the shepherd separates the sheep from the goats; and He will put the sheep on His right, and the goats on the left. Then the King will say to those on His right, 'Come, you who are

blessed of My Father, inherit the kingdom prepared for you from the foundation of the world. For I was hungry, and you gave Me something to eat; I was thirsty, and you gave Me something to drink; I was a stranger, and you invited Me in; naked, and you clothed Me; I was sick, and you visited Me; I was in prison, and you came to Me.'

"Then the righteous will answer Him, 'Lord, when did we see You hungry, and feed You, or thirsty, and give You something to drink? And when did we see You a stranger, and invite You in, or naked, and clothe You? When did we see You sick, or in prison, and come to You?'

"The King will answer and say to them, 'Truly I say to you, to the extent that you did it to one of these brothers of Mine, even the least of them, you did it to Me'" (MT 25: 31–40).

Here below is another parable with a similar message. We know from the afterlife evidence that there is no fiery hell. We also know that eternal damnation cannot happen. But Jesus may indeed have told a story that was something like this, thinking that those who in this lifetime fail to make spiritual progress might after death consign themselves to the outer darkness for a time:

Jesus presented another parable to them, saying, **"The kingdom of heaven may be compared to a man who sowed good seed in his field. But while his men were sleeping, his enemy came and sowed tares among the wheat, and went away. But when the wheat sprouted and bore grain, then the tares became evident also. The slaves of the landowner came and said to him, 'Sir, did you not sow good seed in your field? How then does it have tares?'**

"And he said to them, 'An enemy has done this!'

"The slaves said to him, 'Do you want us, then, to go and gather them up?'

"But he said, 'No; for while you are gathering up the tares, you may uproot the wheat with them. Allow both to grow together until the harvest; and in the time of the harvest I will say to the reapers, 'First gather up the tares and bind them in bundles to burn them up; but gather the wheat into my barn'" (MT 13:24–30).

What follows is Jesus's reported explanation for this parable. From the thought that Jesus Himself sowed the good seed while an imaginary devil sowed the weeds right through to the notion of end times and a blazing furnace, this whole explanation is a later fabrication. By now, you should be spotting the signs:

"And He said, '**The one who sows the good seed is the Son of Man, and the field is the world; and as for the good seed, these are the sons of the kingdom; and the tares are the sons of the evil one; and the enemy who sowed them is the devil, and the harvest is the end of the age; and the reapers are angels. So just as the tares are gathered up and burned with fire, so shall it be at the end of the age. The Son of Man will send forth His angels, and they will gather out of His kingdom all stumbling blocks, and those who commit lawlessness, and will throw them into the furnace of fire; in that place there will be weeping and gnashing of teeth. Then the righteous will shine forth as the sun in the kingdom of their Father. He who has ears, let him hear'**" (MT 13:37–43).

The whole of Matthew 24 is devoted to end-times prophecy (similar passages are in Mark 13 and in Luke 21:8–36). I have read this chapter repeatedly, trying to figure out what Jesus might have said that could have been the basis for so much that is inconsistent with the afterlife evidence and the teachings of Jesus. All I can conclude is that the Bible-builders wanted to tie the Book of Revelation directly back to Jesus, so they cribbed some of its ideas into His Gospels. When Jesus came to teach us how to use our many earth-lifetimes to better grow toward spiritual perfection, it is beyond nonsensical that He ever would have said, **"This gospel of the kingdom shall be preached in the whole world as a testimony to all the nations, and then the end will come"** (MT 24:14), or **"Truly I tell you, this generation will certainly not pass away until all these things have happened"** (MT 24:34). The only part of this whole chapter that rings true is the Lord's assurance that **"Heaven and earth will pass away, but my words will not pass away"** (MT 24:35).

- And then there are references to an appalling barbarism that still is at the core of Christian traditions. There is no evidence that having taken Christian communion makes any spiritual difference, whether on earth or in the afterlife levels. If we want to limit our reading of the Gospels to just what Jesus must have said, then we've got to turn each description of the Last Supper into a convivial farewell to friends in which Jesus asks them to remember Him whenever they dine together. It is impossible now to know whether the passage that follows is a complete addition, or whether it is the corruption of something that Jesus said about His teachings being as essential as food and drink. We may never know. What we do know is that Jesus never said anything like this! To this

day, He likely remains appalled that you might believe that He ever said it:

"So Jesus said to them, **'Truly, truly, I say to you, unless you eat the flesh of the Son of Man and drink His blood, you have no life in yourselves. He who eats My flesh and drinks My blood has eternal life, and I will raise him up on the last day. For My flesh is true food, and My blood is true drink. He who eats My flesh and drinks My blood abides in Me, and I in him. As the living Father sent Me, and I live because of the Father, so he who eats Me, he also will live because of Me. This is the bread which came down out of heaven; not as the fathers ate and died; he who eats this bread will live forever'"** (JN 6:53–58).

- There is a series of important Gospel phrases where Jesus is seen to be using a personal pronoun in a way that is out of character. It seems likely that to first-century people, their shorthand use of "I" or "me" for "my teachings" in reporting the words of Jesus would have seemed harmless. But it is clear to a modern reader, in view of the fact that religious affiliations are irrelevant when it comes to getting into heaven, that in each of these cases what Jesus was really talking about was His teachings:

"I am the way, and the truth, and the life. No one comes to the Father but through me" must actually have been something like **"My teachings are the way, and the truth, and the life. No one comes to the Father but through my teachings"** (JN 14:6).

"I am the resurrection and the life; he who believes in Me will live even if he dies, and everyone who lives and believes in Me will never die" surely was said something more like **"My teachings are the resurrection and the life. He who believes my teachings will live, even if he dies, and everyone who lives and believes my teachings will never die"** (JN 11:25–26). Note here, too, that for Jesus to be referring to His resurrection years before His death is an anachronism that means that we likely should pitch this whole passage as a suspect addition.

"For God so loved the world that He gave His only begotten Son, that whoever believes in Him shall not perish, but have eternal life" has to have been said something more like **"For God so loved the world that He gave His only begotten Son, that whoever believes His teachings shall not perish, but have eternal life"** (JN 3:16).

Correcting all such mistakes is important, since there is no evidence whatsoever for either sacrificial redemption or the notion that only professed Christians will get into heaven.

- Some bits of coal can be spotted by the way they mischaracterize God. The genuine God that both Jesus and the dead describe to us is perfectly loving Spirit and entirely devoid of human failings. The Old Testament God in the minds of those who were constructing the Christian Bible was judgmental and quick to anger. You will see that it is easy to tell the difference!

"What He has seen and heard, of that He testifies; and no one receives His testimony. He who has received His testimony has set his seal to this, that God is true. For He whom God has sent speaks the words of God; for He gives the Spirit without measure. The Father loves the Son and has given all things into His hand. He who believes in the Son has eternal life; but he who does not obey the Son will not see life, but the wrath of God abides on him" (JN 3:32–36).

God has no wrath! Jesus doesn't "give" the Spirit, but rather each human being is part of God as Spirit. The teachings of Jesus are not rules to be obeyed, but rather they are a prescription for living our best eternal lives. And finally, neither God nor Jesus ever is our afterlife judge. Tossing this one is an easy call. And it is important that we toss it. Today I drove past a billboard that depicted a fiery hell and inquired whether passers-by knew where they would be going if they died tonight. That billboard cited

John 3:36, the last sentence in the passage above. This sort of triumphal unleashing of an imaginary vengeful God against people Jesus says that we must only love is one of Christianity's most repugnant fruits.

Finally, here is a passage that we can imagine might have been, at its base, something that Jesus could have said. His efforts to wean people away from their religious superstitions began to cause disruptions within families, and as His time here grew short, you can see in some Gospel passages a little impatience that He hasn't made more progress. He may well have said in exasperation some version of, **"Look, this is going to get a lot harder. Who's with me?"** An exhortation to greater devotion and renewed effort. I don't buy the parts of this that seem ego-related, like **"worthy of me"** and **"for my sake,"** because that simply is not Jesus. His life on earth was an exercise in humility. I don't buy the anachronistic reference to the cross, either. But Jesus could see that His work was disrupting His disciples' personal lives, and He might well have dealt with that problem frankly. Even so, it is nonsensical to do as Christians do so often, and see a passage like this that is reflective of a long-ago moment in time as Jesus prophesying events that might happen thousands of years later.

"Do not think that I came to bring peace on the earth; I did not come to bring peace, but a sword. For I came to set a man against his father and a daughter against her mother, and a daughter-in-law against her mother-in-law; and a man's enemies will be the members of his household.

"He who loves father or mother more than Me is not worthy of Me; and he who loves son or daughter more than Me is not worthy of Me. And he who does not take his cross and follow after Me is not worthy of Me. He who has found his life will lose it, and he who has lost his life for My sake will find it" (MT 10:34–39).

READING THE GOSPELS ATTENTIVELY

We understand now that Jesus is a genuine historical figure. His Gospel words can be studied and verified. So trying to appreciate ever better what it was that the Lord must actually have said, what He meant by it, and how we can apply His words to creating our best eternal lives as we share His truth with all the world can be our lifelong pleasure. The teachings of Jesus in the Gospels are demonstrated now to be the living Word of our infinitely loving God. And it is only when we follow them with joy as the philosophy they are meant to be that we can at last begin to make our best eternal spiritual progress.

APPENDIX II
A BRIEF OVERVIEW OF THE AFTERLIFE EVIDENCE

We have nearly two hundred years of astonishingly varied afterlife evidence. Just as important as the volume and variety of this evidence is the fact that it is so consistent, and when we put it together we begin to glimpse a wonderfully complex and beautiful reality that dwarfs the material universe. Indeed, the greater reality now coming into view might be as much as twenty times the size of our universe! It is all beyond amazing, and far beyond thrilling.

I recommend that you read Victor and Wendy Zammit's important book, *A Lawyer Presents the Evidence for the Afterlife,* and that you also peruse some of the seventy books listed in the annotated bibliography of *The Fun of Dying.* To help you get started, I will here list in no particular order some of the kinds of evidence that I have used in assembling my understanding of death, the afterlife, and the greater reality in which we live:

- ***Communications Received Through Deep-Trance Mediums.*** Deep-trance mediums are able to withdraw from their bodies sufficiently to let the dead use their vocal cords to speak. The testimony of the best evidence received this way is such that if mainstream physicists had not a century ago already been dogmatically materialist, the fact that you will survive your death would long ago have become common knowledge.

- *Communications Received Through Materialization Mediums.* There are mediums who have developed their skills to such an extent that they can go into deep trance and facilitate the production of voices, sounds, and even our loved ones present in the room.

- *Communications Received Through Psychic Mediums.* This is an area where double- and triple-blind scientific studies are possible, and these studies demonstrate that some psychic mediums indeed are in contact with the dead. The work of the best psychic mediums has produced a wealth of interesting and consistent information.

- *Accounts Received Through Automatic Writing.* Sometimes a medium can invite a dead person to write using the medium's hands. I have read a few accounts that were written this way, and have found them to be so consistent with the information that I have assembled from other sources that I consider the ones that I have read to be likely genuine.

- *Channeled Accounts.* Throughout history, there have been mediums who have received in one way or another entire books that they claimed came from dead people, and that purportedly gave us the straight skinny on what is really going on. I have mistrusted most channeled work, so it is a humbling irony that I have written here what I have been told is largely a channeled work. Never say that God does not have a sense of humor.

- *Consciousness Research.* A century ago, mainstream physicists still grappling with quantum mechanics considered the proofs of their survival that the dead had begun to send to us to be a woo-woo bridge too far. In order to be able to ignore the dead, university and peer-reviewed journal gatekeepers established materialism as what they called a "fundamental scientific dogma." To this day, no research scientist who hopes for a university career dares to study anything that might suggest that reality is based in an underlying intelligence. As a result, researchers still labor in vain to find a source of consciousness in the brain. What bits of information they produce are studied by afterlife researchers, but in truth we are coming to know a lot more about consciousness than they do.

- *Deathbed Visions.* Those who are dying will often have extraordinary experiences that include visits from dead loved ones and occasional glimpses of the places where they will be going after death.

- *Accounts by Out-of-Body Travelers.* There is a lot of evidence that we travel out of our bodies during sleep, but to learn to do it while awake is difficult. There are some, though, who have demonstrated an ability to travel out of their bodies at will, and the published accounts by out-of-body travelers are remarkably consistent with the rest of the evidence.

- *General Scientific Research.* From enigmas like dark matter and energy and the Big Bang, through to the troubling fact that "solid" matter is not solid, modern scientific inquiry remains severely hamstrung by its obsession with materialism as a dogma. At the same time, scientific researchers continue to turn out consistent bits of information that help afterlife researchers as we build our increasingly detailed picture of the greater reality.

- *Ghosts and Spirit Possession.* These are areas so repugnant to me that I try not even to think about them, but little by little I have felt forced to investigate the phenomena of ghosts and spirit possession. And, yes, what we learn there fits the overall picture that we are building.

- *Hypnotic Regression.* Some therapists help their patients regress or progress to what appear to be past or future lives, and thereby help them to resolve some psychological ailments. In doing so, they have uncovered some fascinating, and consistent, information.

- *Instrumental Transcommunication (ITC) Including Electronic Voice Phenomena (EVP).* Communicating with the dead by means of computers, tape recorders, telephones, televisions, and various "black box" devices is a very promising area that has yet to bear much fruit, in part because few living researchers are able to devote the necessary time to conducting experiments at the direction of dead researchers. And occasionally, squabbling among living researchers will cause their dead collaborators to withdraw. More recently, we have come to understand that there also are some very bad nonmaterial entities who are trying to keep reliable communication between the living and the dead from ever happening. Knowing what is wrong is half of solving the problem. Expect reliable electronic communication with the dead to be in place before 2030.

- *Near-Death Experiences.* People who have near-death experiences don't go to the places where the dead reside, but they generally travel out of their bodies and they often have remarkable experiences. When we understand that the events depicted in near-death experiences are not indicative of afterlife facts, we can study just the mechanics of NDEs. And there we find information that is entirely consistent with what we have learned from other sources.

- *Past-Life Memories of Children.* Some toddlers appear to have memories of recent past lives that ended violently. These cases seem to me to be less evidence for general reincarnation than they are suggestions of what might perhaps go wrong in the process of transition.

- *Quantum Physics.* The physics of the places where the dead reside is so different from the physics of this level of reality that until good quantum-physics-for-dummies books became available early in this century, afterlife researchers had trouble making sense of it all. It turns out that quantum physics is a kind of plug that connects what we might think of as the mathematics-based physics of this level of reality with the consciousness-based physics that exists in perhaps ninety-five percent of the greater reality that even physicists are aware must exist. Thanks to those who have made the principles of quantum mechanics understandable to people who never got beyond Algebra II, afterlife researchers are coming to understand a lot more about how reality is put together.

- ***Work of Independent Scientists.*** Nearly all researchers in the field of afterlife studies are lawyers, psychologists, and other laypeople. We revere those few trained scientists who during the past century have come across data that suggested there was a lot more going on than what was currently being studied. Despite the strong stigma in scientific circles that still exists against scientists who don't respect the "fundamental dogma" of materialism, and despite the lack of funding for researchers who venture off the materialist reservation, these visionaries have done extraordinary work in fields related to afterlife studies. All such research results of which I am aware are consistent with what has been developed by earnest laypeople.

It will be easier for you to understand what Jesus is asking of us now if you have some basic understanding of the greater reality in which we live, and awareness of the process of spiritual growth that is the primary task and birthright of every person on earth.

APPENDIX III
A BRIEF OVERVIEW OF THE GREATER REALITY

What afterlife researchers have discovered is a lot more than just the happy fact that every human mind is eternal. Because the afterlife is real, our study of it has led us to the amazing discovery of a greater reality that seems to be many times the size of this material universe, and to a new kind of physics that is consciousness-based. To give you even a rudimentary understanding of the whole picture would take a separate book. Here, I will just share with you brief descriptions of some of the aspects of the afterlife on which researchers generally agree, in an effort to make it easier for you to better understand what Jesus is saying.

GOD

The human-like God that Christians worship does not exist. Instead, the only thing that exists is an energy-like potentiality without size or form, infinitely powerful, alive in the sense that your mind is alive, highly emotional and therefore probably self-aware. And the only emotion this genuine God expresses is love beyond our ability to comprehend it. Each human mind is part of God. It is likely not wrong to say that God and all our minds together are of an energy that we experience as consciousness, but no one knows much about God beyond the definition given above. Everything that we think of as real is an aspect or an artifact of God. And creation, if you want to call it that, is apparently not a one-time thing. Evidence suggests that God is continuously manifesting the reality that we believe exists around us.

THE STRUCTURE OF THE GREATER REALITY

The simplest way to envision reality is as a spectrum of energy signals very much like the television signals that are in the room around you, and to imagine your mind as a television set now tuned to that particular body on this material level of reality. We think this is the lowest vibratory level, but no one is sure about that. We do know that existing at slightly higher vibratory rates are at least seven levels of nonmaterial reality that we think of as our afterlife levels. Each of them may be as big as this whole material universe, and all of them, like the TV signals in the room around you, are together in one place.

176

Nothing is solid. Everything is energy. The only thing that objectively exists is God, and every human mind is an infinitely loved part of God.

THE AFTERLIFE LEVELS

There are at least seven energy-based post-death levels of reality. Six of them feel as solid to their inhabitants as this material level feels to us, and all of them are in the same place, just as you can tune your TV from a lower channel to a higher channel and find there a different TV program. We can be comfortable on the highest afterlife level to which our personal degree of spiritual development suits us, but we find it unbearable to go higher. And we want to go higher! There is more to do, there are ever more pleasures on the higher vibratory levels. So the more spiritual progress you can make in this lifetime, the more kinds of fun will be available to you later.

Right above the vibratory rate of matter is the lowest afterlife level, what Jesus called the outer darkness. It is the punishment level, cold and dark, smelly and repellent and populated by tormented, demon-like people. Just above the first level is a recovery level, still twilight-dark, but with homes and without the awful cold and stench and hopelessness of the lowest level.

Levels Three through Five of the afterlife are the beautiful Summerland levels. All three are intensely earthlike, full of flowers in extraordinary colors and magnificent buildings and scenery. The higher the vibratory rate of each of these levels, the more gorgeous everything appears to be.

Level Six is just below the Source. Historically the dead have called it the causal or mental level, since it is the home of spiritually advanced people who mind-create what exists in the lower afterlife levels. (I recall long ago reading an account from a sixth-level being who was frustrated by the process of learning how to create living plants. It was hilarious.) A friend of mine who died in 2007 and now lives in the sixth level refers to it as the teaching level, since for many who live at that level, spiritual teaching in the lower afterlife levels and on earth is a primary occupation. He tells us that the sixth level is full of beautiful universities where very advanced beings help one another to make ever more spiritual progress.

The highest vibratory level of which we are aware is the Celestial or Source Level, which is something like the center of God. It exists at such a high spiritual vibratory rate that it seems that very few of us have yet been able to enter it. The Celestial Level is the source of the magnificent white light that fills most of the greater reality and makes it feel to those who are there as if they are living bathed in love.

THE DEATH PROCESS

Our bodies resist dying. Getting them to the point where they can no longer support life and we are released from these earthly shells can be a rough experience, as I have been reminded by some who objected to the title of my book, *The Fun of Dying*. But shortly before we leave our bodies, the fun begins as we start to see some of those we had loved in life and thought were dead come crowding around our deathbed. We leave our bodies as what might appear to bedside observers to be an energy mist, and we reform into a human shape while still attached to our material body by a spiritual umbilicus called the silver cord. This process of liberation is quite pleasurable, as is our joyous reunion with loved ones at our bedside. We might hardly notice the fraying of our silver cord, but once it is severed, the physical body dies. Then we are off with those we love, raising our spiritual vibratory rate to the point where a whole new solid and beautiful reality appears around us. If you will trust in the process, you will find that dying is just that easy, and just that wonderful.

OUR POST-DEATH LIFE

A whole book by itself could be written about all that the dead have been pleased to tell us about their wonderful post-death lives. Here are a few highlights:

Our bodies are mind-created, and most of us choose to look and feel as we did while on earth at maybe age thirty. The standard "spirit robe" is a long-sleeved, floor-length belted tunic in vibrant pastel hues, like an angel's dress; but many people prefer to wear earth-clothing. Nobody cares how you dress. My sixth-level friend who died in 2007 at the age of 20 tells us that he wears college-kid clothes most of the time, but when he returns to the sixth level he wears his spirit robe.

Dead children are treated like royalty, reared in beautiful homes and villages that are off-limits to any but their carefully-selected caretakers. They grow to young adulthood at their own pace, generally over just a few earth-years, and they closely follow their parents' lives and greet their eventual arrival with joy. Even miscarried and aborted babies grow up here and lovingly greet their parents. I recall one early-twentieth-century communication in which a woman who apparently had had several coat-hanger abortions reported having been staggered to be greeted by beautiful young adults who loved her and called her their mother.

There are infinite things to do. And since night never falls and we don't need to sleep, we have close to infinite time in which to do them. We travel in space and travel in time, play sports, learn to paint and play the piano, research our past lives, attend Elvis concerts, take classes, boat and fly around, show up at impromptu welcoming parties, and even sit at the feet of Jesus. My sixth-level friend spends a lot of time snowboarding. The more spiritually advanced you are, the more options are available to you, which is another reason to take your earthly spiritual growth seriously.

All the companion animals we have loved in life are there to greet us, now young and healthy. Apparently animals have species-specific "group souls" to which they return at death, but being loved by a human being enables them to establish an independent existence. They live in the afterlife in happy packs, or they live with your family members until you arrive. Like us, they neither eat nor eliminate, so the only care that they need now is love.

And yes, I do understand that all of this seems too good to be true. You are coming home for milk and cookies and comfort after your rough day in school, and what you get is a three-ring circus of ponies and elephants and aerial acts and every earthly pleasure. As I have read so many wonderful accounts, sometimes I could envision the heavenly host sort of chortling together with glee as they thought up ever more treats that you in particular might enjoy. It is impossible for you to grasp the infinite extent to which you are perfectly loved.

APPENDIX IV
EXPERIENCES OF LIGHT

My lifelong interest in death is an offshoot of something that happened in April of 1955. One morning I woke up just before dawn and was struck by the thought that there is no God. I stared in terror into the darkness, too full of despair even to seek the comfort of my parents' bed. What comfort can there be if there is no God?

Suddenly there was a flash of white light in the room. I could look at it without squinting, and even sixty years later I still recall the wonder of seeing light shining on my toy horse, on my plastic dolls in a row, on that awful lavender wallpaper. In the midst of the flash, I heard a young male voice say, **"You wouldn't know what it is to have me unless you knew what it is to be without me. I will never leave you again."**

Almost forty years went by before I told anyone what had happened to me, but it shaped my growing-up. Surely my experience had been normal. I assumed that I was going to learn about experiences of light at church or in school or somewhere. I even majored in religion in college, but of course all that I learned in college was what the world's religions had taught. By my junior year, I was starting to think that my experience would be a mystery forever. Then, one August day as I was turning twenty, I came home from my summer job and sat down on my bed, feeling glum.

Suddenly there it was again, that magnesium-white light filling the room, this time accompanied by indescribable music. Think of a thousand tiny bells playing beautifully and loudly. Then came that same young male voice, this time saying only, **"I will never leave you."**

Never for a minute since that day have I thought that I was alone, and never have I doubted the existence of God. And for many years, I was convinced that I was the literal dunce of the universe, since God had to make His point to me twice. I was so embarrassed that for years I swore to God that I always would remember that He was real, **"so please don't ever do that to me again!"** In all the years since, God never has.

For nearly four decades I lived with the thought that the only three people who had been spoken to out of a flash of light were Moses, the Apostle Paul, and a dumbfounded American child.

Here is what happened to Moses:

"The angel of the Lord appeared to him in a blazing fire from the midst of a bush; and he looked, and behold, the bush was burning with fire, yet the bush was not consumed. So Moses said, **'I must turn aside now and see this marvelous sight, why the bush is not burned up.'**

"When the Lord saw that he turned aside to look, God called to him from the midst of the bush and said, **'Moses, Moses!'**

"And he said, **'Here I am.'**

"Then He said, **'Do not come near here; remove your sandals from your feet, for the place on which you are standing is holy ground'**" (Exodus 3:2–5).

And here is how a zealot named Saul was converted after the death of Jesus from a persecutor of those who had followed the Lord into the Apostle Paul, the architect of the early Church:

"Now Saul, still breathing threats and murder against the disciples of the Lord, went to the high priest, and asked for letters from him to the synagogues at Damascus, so that if he found any belonging to the Way, both men and women, he might bring them bound to Jerusalem. As he was traveling, it happened that he was approaching Damascus, and suddenly a light from heaven flashed around him; and he fell to the ground and heard a voice saying to him, **'Saul, Saul, why are you persecuting Me?'**

"And he said, **'Who are You, Lord?'**

"And He said, **'I am Jesus whom you are persecuting, but get up and enter the city, and it will be told you what you must do'"** (Acts 9:1–6).

These great religious figures had conversed with the voices they had heard from the light. For my part, when I saw the light and heard the voice, my only thought was that it was handy that if you forget there is a God, they remind you. But until I was forty-five, I never heard of anyone else outside the Bible who had had an experience of light.

Then my father had a major stroke. For the two weeks that he survived, I made a daily round trip to be with my parents, and on one of those nights my mother had essentially my same experience. She saw a flash of white light, and a voice said, **"I'm giving you a few more days with him so you can get a few things straight."**

(Nobody said these great experiences have to be poetic.)

It was only after I discovered that they had not been unique to me that I began to mention my experiences of light. I have found that a few of those with whom I have shared my experiences have had similar experiences themselves, and they generally don't talk about them, either. This is something so personal, so extraordinary, and frankly so weird that you don't talk about it. But it is something that stays in your mind. I have no other memories from the spring when I was eight, but still that predawn minute shines.

As to what makes an experience of light look and sound as it does, here are my thoughts:

- All the post-death levels exist right here, and the third level and above are filled with a white light that is brighter than sunlight. Opening a portal between our levels might leak that light through briefly, which I have come to think is what happens.

- Most people who have experiences of light have the same sense that I did: the light is in the room, but the voice and music may be in your mind.

- Experiences of light seem to occur when we are under some spiritual strain, and most of the messages that have been shared with me were spiritual in nature.

- People differ on who it was they thought they heard speaking, and by their descriptions I have come to guess that we all hear different voices.

The voice that I heard was young and male and it didn't seem quite God-like, so when in my research I encountered spirit guides, I realized that my voice must have been my spirit guide. My mother was certain that she had heard the literal voice of God Himself, and I find it interesting that as her brain deteriorated with end-stage senile dementia, her experience of light was the last thing she forgot, even when she no longer recognized her children.

- To hear a voice in your mind as clearly as you hear spoken words is a remarkable experience. I assure you that you can tell the difference between spoken words and your own thoughts. No question.

Having lived successfully for decades after I had my last experience of light, having married and reared children and practiced law and made friends, I am demonstrably not crazy. But I am so glad that at the age of eight I knew enough not to tell anyone what had happened to me! Now I wonder how many others have been made to consider themselves insane because they had this sort of wonderful cross-dimensional message, and the doctors they trusted with it decided that they had to be mad. I have come to think that many things that mainstream scientists still find puzzling may have their origins in the afterlife levels, which is another reason why I hope that soon they can get past their beliefs-based views of what reality must be.

APPENDIX V
HOW THIS BOOK CAME TO BE WRITTEN

If learning that an American Founding Father and the Son of the Living God have asked me to help them save the world is going to make your head explode, please skip this Appendix. On the other hand, if you are curious to discover where giving your life to God might lead you, read on . . .

All of us have spirit guides who help us to live the life-plans that we made before we were born. It must have been my primary guide who spoke to me when I was eight, but in all the sixty years since that night I never had wanted a daytime meeting with him. We travel out of body during sleep, and we often meet with our spirit guides. I always had felt well-guided.

Then on February 21, 2015, I had a telephone reading with Susanne Wilson. It was my first attempt to visit with my dead family members in more than a decade. After I had done extensive research with spiritual mediums in the nineties and in the early oughts, I had come to the conclusion that most mediums have marginal gifts and

191

many may be outright charlatans. Susanne, however, had come well-recommended. And I had had the growing sense that my mother was trying to get in touch with me, since we hadn't yet connected following her death in July of 2012. So I entered that reading feeling positive, and I received a series of wonderful validations that included small, peculiar things that only my parents could have known. It was a great reading. I was delighted and uplifted and laughing again with people I had missed so much.

My intention had been just to visit my family, but toward the end of the hour my spirit guides asked to speak with me. I learned on that Saturday afternoon that I have eleven guides. Four of them help with my personal life, three work with me on writing fiction, and three assist with my afterlife-related projects. And then my primary guide stepped forward and announced that his name is Thomas. In his penultimate earth-lifetime, he had been—imagine a drumroll—Thomas Jefferson.

I was less dumbfounded when I first heard this than you might expect. I have had for my entire life an intense affinity for Thomas Jefferson, even to the point of writing a well-received novel about his ten-year marriage. Being a primary guide is a full-time job, and of course I felt unworthy of that kind of attention from someone I idolized, but he insisted during our first reading that I not think of him as Thomas Jefferson. That hadn't even been his most recent lifetime. He told Susanne that he had still been evolving during his lifetime as Jefferson. It might have been his last earth-lifetime, but he told her he had had too much power and he hadn't always used it well.

Okay then. Thank you. Isn't life amazing?

I was still sharing with friends the curious anecdote that my primary guide is Thomas Jefferson and just kind of giggling about it when on a Thursday in May I received an email from Susanne. She said that Thomas wanted to speak with me. She had a little time on Saturday. Would I like to hear what he had to say?

So on May 16th I spent an intense hour listening and arguing. This reading was so life-changing for me that I am going to quote from it liberally.

Thomas began by saying through Susanne, **"Corruption of all the Master taught continues now. This is the blockage of the port through which peace must sail freely. Hearts are not free."**

As my other guides filed into the heavenly conference room where Thomas was talking with Susanne, she said to me, **"You're curious about the relationships you've had with him before. There are seventeen lives in which you've known each other. In most of them you were** someone involved in a church, and he was trying to keep it from being so stubborn and dogmatic and corrupt. He keeps saying the Church has always been corrupt. Throughout history."

Susanne made it clear that by "corrupt," Thomas meant the corruption of the Master's message. She said, **"Thomas is part of the Unity—this group of souls that works to give support and encouragement to people here who are working to advance consciousness. It has to do with world peace. In every life he's had he has been misrepresented and misunderstood, and that's fine with him. He says, 'In the controversy is the healing.' He's calling you 'my daughter.'"**

Thomas was surprisingly negative about his lifetime as an American hero. Susanne said, **"He was not proud of his presidency. It's the ugliness of the insincere men around him. He also says, 'I could have done more.' He sought balance and fairness. He saw his opportunity, and there were things he wished would have been different. He didn't want attention for himself, he eschewed the celebrity aspect, but he wanted to use it.**

"People called him an atheist. That's the only thing that bothered him. He is not unhappy with the way he is perceived now. He admits that he was. He thought he would get a lot more done."

Thomas told Susanne that his lifetime as Jefferson had so unbalanced him spiritually that he had needed to live one further lifetime as a farmer in Wales. His son in that lifetime had been a clergyman, and again Thomas had been trying to reform Christianity.

But I wasn't interested in any of that. I was still focused on my hero. For decades my office centerpiece has been a life-sized bust of Thomas Jefferson, for heaven's sake! I found myself arguing with the man himself that he had to help me write a book that would defend his Jefferson lifetime against all the lies.

"I know why you didn't free your slaves! I know who was the real father of Sally Hemings's children! It's time to fight the slanders, Thomas!"

Susanne told me he didn't care about any of that now. I was missing the point! I was supposed to be passionate about the mission, not the man.

"He just wants the work done. He wants you to know you're already doing it. It's about the teachings of Jesus! That's his agenda! There's something about a book of his that was lost. He can dictate it to you. It's to be about Jesus. But it should be written from your perspective, for this modern day.

"The real Jesus, not the Christian Jesus. That is corrupted. They corrupted the teachings of Jesus. He's

saying the Master has asked this of you. So it's not just Thomas. He's showing me a book, and the word Jesus is on the front of the book. And it has to do with the philosophy. You already have it written! Just go through and bring together everything you've written about the Master and His teaching. There's more that will be flowing through your pen. You'll find that you can weave it all together seamlessly in a narrative. You're going to create Thomas's lost book, but in a modern version. You have helped him with his life's story. (I assume he meant my novel, *My Thomas*.) Now it's time for the Master. If you can help Thomas do this, then his work will be complete. And your thirst for 'What can I do for Thomas?' shall be quenched."

I sputtered, "But I want to keep him from being misjudged! I know why he owned slaves! I know who was the real father—!"

"He's saying, 'Don't you see? If we can raise the consciousness, none of that will matter! We're working for peace.' If you can get this done for him, that will help him, too."

Um, okay. I sat briefly, thinking. I said, "I'll do my best. I just don't know how it will all come together."

"He says, 'Beautifully.'"

Then Susanne said, **"Now he's showing me these political ads on television. He's saying, 'Can you imagine what they would say about me?' He's chuckling."**

I said something sulky about thinking it wasn't all that funny. Susanne said, **"You're focused on having him be understood. He's just focused on getting his work carried through."**

Then her tone changed. She said, **"He sees . . . I'm being shown two hundred years from now. Some kind of religious war . . . small populations . . . we have fewer people in the world. Part of what he is asking you to do is more important than you might think because it can help prevent this religious war. There are fewer people on the earth plane because many people have lost the ability to reproduce. And all the food is manufactured. The Christians—Thomas calls them the 'so-called Christians'—caused the war because of their corruption of Jesus. He says, 'We're working to prevent this war! This is a possible future to be prevented.' Now the curtains close, then open, and there is a new movie. I think I'm looking at heaven because of the way the flowers are. They seem alive. I can see them growing. Oh—no. He says this is the other possibility. Heaven on** earth! He says, 'Many of us work diligently with many of you. Together we prevail!'"

I remarked that he seemed to be trying to rescue Jesus from Christianity.

Susanne said, **"Whoa, that's the mission! That is the mission!"**

But who was Jesus, anyway? I told Susanne that He must have been a very advanced ascended being. She listened to Thomas, and then said, **"Many people think Jesus was that, or was an avatar. But Jesus was a man! He was made flesh so the world has the opportunity to understand, and so God has the opportunity to feel the human nature. It was a learning exercise for God, too. It wasn't just Jesus helping us. It was part of God's exercise to understand how the freedom we were given went so wrong."**

"So Jesus really was a form of divinity?"

"Thomas says yes! We're all part of God, but Jesus came from the highest part of God. God looked right through His eyes. We think of earth as our school, but it's also God's school. God was learning about us."

I was beginning to wonder how I might do this. Before I could ask the question, Susanne said, **"When you start pulling together all these pieces of things you already have written, it will start to flow for you. It won't be** ambiguous. **It will be quite clear. What we would call the hook in terms of marketing will be tying in your afterlife research with the epiphany of the Man and his teachings. Thomas keeps using the word 'philosophy.'"**

I said, **"So they're saying we have to do this now to prevent the war two hundred years from now?"** I was struggling to get my mind around how I might have been chosen to do something so important.

"Yes, but don't think the weight of the world is on your shoulders. There are many people working on this."

"They won't let me screw it up?"

"They're telling me a mistake is impossible."

* * *

The next morning was a Sunday. I had a little time, so I started writing. There seemed to be a table of contents in my mind. There was a title, *Liberating Jesus*, which sounded clumsy to me. Let's make it *Freeing Jesus!* What about that? The thought came: **No.**

Soon I was into writing an author's preface, then an introduction, then a first chapter. Ideas appeared in my mind. I wrote them down. I would stop every so often and gather more of my blog posts and other tidbits that I had written about Jesus and see where they might fit in. It felt easy. And it was fun!

But I guess it wasn't happening fast enough. After all, I still was practicing law and finishing a novel and living my life. Soon it was almost a whole month later, and so far I had only three chapters written. So on the evening of June 9th, Susanne emailed me to say that Thomas had just seized her briefly in a Walmart parking lot and said, **"Please forgive the speed at which we are dictating, as your soul-ular self is working directly for the Master now, without benefit of the filters which would slow the transmission. And I hasten to add, you must please of course speak clearly should your physical suffer exhaustion."**

Susanne added, **"That was amazing. Thomas is an unassuming man. Very calm and personable. I doubt he suffers fools, though. No nonsense. He's removing all obstacles to get this book published and known. He gave that message through trance mediumship. I was him for a minute."**

* * *

Wow. Fascinating. But what did it mean?

At two o'clock the next morning, I began to discover what it meant. I often wake up in the middle of the night and write for a while, so my waking up then didn't feel surprising. But as soon as I sat down at my computer, I felt as if I had stepped from a Ford into a Maserati. I was revamping the table of contents, rewriting those first three chapters, redoing the whole concept of the fourth chapter and writing nearly all of that, then slogging all the rest of what I had already written about Jesus in behind the rest of the new chapter titles. I never managed to make it back to bed. I wrote all night and then all day.

My husband deserved a little time, too. By nine o'clock, I was exhausted. I couldn't ever do that again. I said in my mind, **"Jesus, I really need to sleep! Please don't wake me up until after four, at least!"**

When I woke up the next morning and looked at my bedside clock, it was 4:01. I got up then and worked for a bit. I went into the kitchen at six, where I found that the clock on the oven also said 4:01. By the time my husband got up, that clock was showing a normal time. Delivering meaningful numbers on digital clocks is a common sign from the dead, and apparently Jesus has a sense of humor.

* * *

I don't know what channeling is supposed to feel like, and I thought I was shaping most of the words, but ideas would form without effort and in the right order and I'd be scrambling to get them fully written down. Often I would find myself back randomly reading what I had written earlier and not knowing why and trying to move on, but then I'd be back and rereading repeatedly until I noticed something that apparently I was supposed to fix. There were times when I would try to write when the ideas weren't appearing in my mind. Perhaps Jesus was on a break? Inevitably, whatever I had written without Him would need to be rewritten. So, was this channeling? I have no idea. I only know that having the writing flow this way is the most fun that you can imagine.

I thought there wasn't much of a change in energy between Thomas and Jesus. I felt zippier, but not uncomfortably so. The primary difference seemed to be that Jesus was piling it on me, day and night, so all I wanted to do was write. Soon, though, I was off on a weeklong business trip during which I had no time to write. That pressure of ideas was always there, and it made me unbelievably cranky. At the end of my trip, I shared breakfast with Jamie Turndorf, radio's Dr. Love, who is a dear friend of mine. She is psychic. And when I snipped at her that her efforts to cheer me up were not helping, and I even griped that Jesus had forgotten that people still in bodies have jobs, she put her finger on my problem. She said, **"Stop it! You're letting your ego fight with Him. Get your ego out of the way. This is not about you!"**

OMG, as the teenagers say. After a long heart-to-heart with my sympathetic friend, I realized that the interruption in my writing had led me to an ego-fueled panic. I had become afraid of even attempting to write with Him again. It was all ego. She talked me down from it. When I got on the plane the next morning to head home, my Friend was there and waiting to begin. Soon, we were happily back at work.

* * *

Jesus seems to feel strongly about many things. I would think a question as I was writing, and immediately get an emphatic answer. What about using some of the other Gospels, too? **NO.** Maybe a quote from Mahatma Gandhi? **NO.** Martin Luther King? **NO.** Let's show them how to fix Christianity? **NO.** What about tailoring this to include other religions? **NO.** I would go back and reread some of what I had written and want to soften it a bit here and there, but **NO** would be emphatic in my mind. I was telling close friends that, wow, Jesus was angry, but it wasn't anger. It was determination. He was emphatic about using just the four canonical Gospels, corrected for corruptions but changed as little as possible. Eventually I began to hear what seemed to be bits of His thoughts in my mind. **"It is enough."** And **"I can use this."** And **"It's time for those who love Me to read My words."** And **"Put your heart where your mouth is."**

I really don't want to name my Collaborator! The ideas stand on their own just fine. And my ego squirms at the thought of claiming that, you know, Jesus is talking to me. (Oh. He just said, **"I'm not talking to you. I'm talking to them."** I needed that reminder.)

I am not a theologian, but I majored in religion in college with an emphasis in early Christianity. I grew up devoutly Protestant, then converted to Catholicism as a young adult. I have taught both versions of Sunday school. For many years I was a Catholic Lector. I have read the Christian Bible through repeatedly, and I've read the Gospels so many times that I can quote whole passages. So everything that Jesus needed to use in writing this book was in my mind somewhere. All He had to do was make me think of it.

As I write this Appendix, Jesus keeps prompting me to use the words **"second revelation"** or **"new revelation."** His first attempt two thousand years ago to teach us these essential truths was His first revelation. He made it simple, but still those to whom He spoke were too stuck in first-century religious fears to really grasp what He was saying. Then He tried again to speak to us in the nineteen-sixties by leading the group behind *A Course in Miracles*. Sadly, that beautiful work is so far above our heads that it was another miss. So this time He is speaking directly to Christians, using our own language and our own Scriptures. He is giving us a challenge. **"You say you're following Me? Then *listen* to Me."**

* * *

I have learned so much in the course of writing this book! And I certainly have learned humility. I have come to realize that this experience of being given ideas so I could write them down was just an extension of what I have been doing for the whole latter part of my life. Night after night, while my body slept I would sit at that heavenly table and be educated about how the afterlife evidence that I was reading could be made to fit together, and then later on I was shown how beautifully it all fit with the teachings of Jesus. I would wake up each morning, feeling clever, and begin to write down what I was learning in teaching materials and blog posts and eventually in *The Fun of*

Dying. It was a slap-your-head moment when I first understood that I had done none of this on my own.

Indeed, I now see that my whole life has been lived in preparation for writing this book. But when the time came to actually do what I had long ago agreed to do, apparently I chickened out. My guides must have been trying for a while to psyche me into re-creating Thomas Jefferson's book about Jesus, but I wasn't doing it. I never would have had the nerve to do it if I had believed it was my own idea. So eventually, Thomas became sufficiently exasperated to break into my daytime life and tell me who he was and what I was supposed to do now. With the threat of Armageddon added into the bargain.

The Gospel teachings of Jesus are our surest route to rapid spiritual growth. Until we actually begin to live by the philosophy that Jesus taught, humankind will continue to flounder. More generations will be born and die while making too little spiritual progress, and we will spiral toward the religious war that was predicted long ago in a madman's ravings. God's Kingdom on earth still is possible! But it requires that we leave religious dogmas behind as the spiritual crutch that they are so we can work together to elevate humankind toward God's level of awareness. Jesus is calling upon Christians now to spread His teachings to the modern world. And if you have read this far, then perhaps He is in particular calling to you.

"When He saw the crowds, He had compassion on them, because they were harassed and helpless, like sheep without a shepherd. Then He said to His disciples, **'The harvest is plentiful but the workers are few. Ask the Lord of the harvest, therefore, to send out workers into his harvest field'"** (MT 9:36–38).

23284913R00128

Printed in Great Britain
by Amazon